Praise for Se

"I have had the opportunity to work with Mike on several occasions and his knowledge and expertise on sales, sales approaches, and best methods is some of the best I have seen. He has a tremendous amount of experience and practical wisdom that is extremely valuable to any organization. In addition, his unique content and approach to training our sales team and in the delivery of successful sales models is a huge benefit to our team and organization that will yield a great deal of success for years to come."

— Steve Dusek, President, Dakota Business Lending

"If I were still leading an organization, "Sell like a Monk…" would be a book I would challenge my sales team to study. It reminds me of the St. Thomas Aquinas definition of love… 'to will the good of the other'. Seems to me that's exactly the approach a Monk would take.

Dina Dwyer-Owens, author of *Values Inc.*; motivational speaker and past CEO and Chair of Neighborly

"I've been through many sales seminars and workshops over my 25+ year sales career. The information you present in your book is the most time I have invested in learning because it is person centric, it is using my strengths and seems custom built for me. I cannot wait to put it into action!"

–Ryan Welsh, Director of Marketing, Growth Energy

SELL LIKE A MONK

Wisdom
Editions
Minneapolis

FIRST CALUMET EDITION APRIL 2023
Sell Like a Monk: Timeless Rules for Modern Selling.
Copyright © 2023 by Mike Ferrell. All rights reserved.

10 9 8 7 6 5 4 3 2
ISBN: 978-1-960250-81-0

Cover and interior design: Gary Lindberg

principledflourishing.com

SELL LIKE
A MONK

TIMELESS RULES FOR
MODERN SELLING

Mike Ferrell

Wisdom
Editions
Minneapolis

Table of Contents

your story

Also by
Mike Ferrell

Ultimate Breakthrough Planning:
The Business Funnel Approach

The Sweet Spot:
Where Business Strategy, Positive Psychology
and Faith Principles Converge

Introduction

"What haven't you done?" That's a very common question I get when people hear about my journey. The journey has had a few twists and turns, from golf pro to studying for the priesthood to teacher to entrepreneur to business coach and consultant to author and now a husband, stepdad, grandpa and Benedictine Oblate. A thirst for learning has led me to try many things, and the journey has helped me understand what it takes to go from success to impact.

I grew up watching my father build a successful financial planning business. Because of that experience, I had always wanted to build a business. After graduating from St. John Vianney Seminary and the University of St. Thomas in education, and then teaching and administrating in Catholic education for two years, I decided to make the jump into entrepreneurship.

In 1987, I started my first business and have been building businesses for over thirty years. Of the fourteen start-ups I have been part of, not all have been successful. I've learned much more from the failures, however, than I did from the successes. I was the co-founder of a successful insurance brokerage company, one of the first in the industry to solely focus on alternative distribution channels. With that rewarding experience, I went on to consult and coach hundreds of agents, advisors, agencies and banks.

Three salespeople that were the best at what they did influenced me and this book is dedicated to them. The first of these was my dad, who, for over fifty years, worked in the financial services business as a financial advisor. He taught me the importance of taking care of his clients; he would bend over backward to make sure his clients were taken care of. After he passed away in 2009, I had the opportunity to serve some of those clients, and they would often tell me about my dad's dedication to their best interests. When I started in the financial services industry, Dad told me, "Remember who writes the commission checks. It's your clients that write your commission checks, not the insurance companies. Don't trust those bastards!"

The second person who most influenced me was Bob Faehn. Bob had spent years as a radio broadcaster, station manager, sales manager, salesman and station owner. He was the consummate sales professional, always looking for a win-win situation and never pushing customers into doing things they weren't comfortable doing. As a manager, he always gave his salespeople the support and tools they needed to succeed, allowed them to be their own best selves and was always there to pick them up when they failed. It's probably why many of his salespeople stayed with him for over twenty years. He and I spent many wine sessions talking about sales strategies and business success. Bob died of cancer just over a year ago, which was heartbreaking for me because he wanted to see me finish this book.

My wife Anne is the third most influential person in my life, the one I still get to see in sales every day. She is a realtor, one of the best I've ever known. She goes to great lengths to make sure her clients get a wonderful customer experience. That's probably why 95 percent of her clients are either repeats or referrals. She is also a joyful person and exercises, better than anyone else I know, the positive sales behaviors I talk about in a later chapter.

If you're wondering why I am qualified to write this book, here are some additional bona fides. For more than thirty years, I've worked in over forty different industries with over four thousand salespeople. My clients have included Fortune 500 companies like Transamerica, Nationwide Insurance and Bank of America. In addition, I've worked with many mid-size broker-dealers in the country and their financial advisors and hundreds of small to mid-size businesses. I've been involved in selling since I was in eighth grade when I sold paint and hardware at my parent's store. I've sold golf clubs, financial services, food, wine, shoes, canvas bags, Velcro and hockey equipment. In addition, I have done significant research on sales success and what that looks like. On my bookcases are over a hundred books on selling. I have attended numerous training sessions and workshops about sales success, all in the service of providing my clients the edge needed to succeed.

What I have observed in sales training over these past thirty years is that there are many good training programs, books and speakers, but almost always, each of them focuses on one primary area, such as sales tactics, sales motivation or the inner game of selling. But what I have not found is a book or training program that puts it all together—a comprehensive system that encompasses every aspect of successful selling. A process that can truly transform how they do business and how to succeed.

This, then, is the goal of *Sell Like a Monk*. A lofty goal? Yes, but one that is greatly needed in today's complex world of selling.

Chapter 1
How Can a Monk Help
You with Sales?

What if we have it wrong? For many decades, sales have been about performance-driven results. It's been what many call a "numbers game"—if we make enough calls, have enough appointments, do enough presentations and close enough sales, we'll be successful. Those goal metrics are generally gleaned from previous successful patterns. This theory claims that if we replicate the numbers, then we'll be successful, and if we're successful, we'll be happy.

This approach has led to two crises. One is that turnover in most sales professions is extremely high. Over 80 percent of realtors don't survive their first five years, and over 94 percent of financial advisors won't survive their first two years. According to

Hubspot, the average turnover for salespeople in all industries is somewhere between 35 and 40 percent, which is three times higher than all other professions.

In addition, over the last few years—especially post-COVID—we have experienced a mental health crisis in sales professions. A recent study by the Sales Health Alliance indicates that mental health is a big problem in sales today. According to this study, the three primary drivers of mental health problems in salespeople are:

- Micro-management by sales managers.

- Missing sales targets.

- Working with de-motivated salespeople.

The "by the numbers" sales process also encourages competition against others in the same organization and competition against competitors. In other words, this persistent pursuit of results focuses on beating someone or something. This has characterized the selling profession for decades. Sales management and sales training processes have revolved around the concept. Consequently, we keep making the same mistakes. Doing the same things and expecting different results is the definition of insanity.

What would happen if selling was more about being virtuous, about making people happy, about using your God-given gifts, strengths and talents to achieve excellence *and joy* in your career? What if our work started with us being happy? What if our work was about competing against ourselves so that each day we would become better at what we do and leave our work and organizations in a better place than they were the day before? In his book *The Happiness Advantage*, author Shawn Achor wrote:

> For untold generations now we've been led to believe that happiness orbited around success. That is, if we work hard enough, we will be successful, and only if we are successful will we be happy. Success was thought to be a fixed point in the universe, with happiness revolving around it… We're now learning that the opposite is true, when we are happy, when our mindset and mood are positive, we are smarter, more motivated, and thus more successful.

He goes on to say that happy people are more productive, more engaged at work, generate more sales, and make more money. Happiness leads to success in nearly every domain of our lives—marriage, health, friendship, community involvement, creativity, and in our work.

In 1998, I wrote a paper called "Sales Development vs. Sales Training: A Different Approach." This paper caused quite a stir in the financial services industry because it was completely opposite of many practices in the industry. The paper pointed out that companies spend billions of dollars on sales training but very little on sales development. In other words, most companies focus on the *tactics* of selling, not on *developing the person*.

In 2018, when I was first introduced to the *Rule of Benedict* and its key principles, I dug out that old paper and found that many principles of the *Rule* could directly correlate with sales development. This eventually resulted in the book you are reading, *Sell Like a Monk: Timeless Rules for Modern Selling*.

Over my fifty years of selling and working with salespeople, I've made some important discoveries about the sales profession.

- **Sales is hard work and made even harder by poor management.**

- **Great salespeople rarely make great sales managers.**

- **Successful salespeople—the high performers—cannot be cloned.**

- **Salespeople without a plan and process fail no matter how hard they work.**

- **Most sales organizations and businesses create cookie-cutter sales plans and processes that mostly don't work.**

- **There is no perfect type of person that excels in sales.**

As we have learned, most companies boil sales

down to a numbers game. They have spent years fine-tuning their numbers and believe they can predict what a salesperson will accomplish if they adopt the prescribed pattern of behavior. Unfortunately, they seem to forget the wild card in the system—people. And people are very unpredictable. Repeatedly, I've seen salespeople do all the right things and fail. I've seen salespeople who were declared as least likely to succeed go on to excel dramatically. A second mistake made by many companies is to believe that if they train their salespeople on specific tactics and those people faithfully execute those tactics, predictable results will follow.

What makes salespeople successful varies dramatically depending on the salesperson. Consider this quote from James Clear, author of *Atomic Habits,* because the exact same thing can be said about salespeople:

> Asking what makes someone successful is like asking which ingredient makes a recipe taste good. It's not any single ingredient. It is the combination of many ingredients in the right proportions and in the right order—and the absence of anything that would ruin the mixture.

Unfortunately, most sales organizations think the recipe for great salespeople is the same for *every* person. In my experience with thousands of salespeople, that is the wrong approach.

The US military calls our contemporary sales environment VUCA—volatile, uncertain, complex and ambiguous. This ever-changing environment has been made even more difficult because of pandemics, social unrest, political uncertainty and economic instability. Salespeople today must deal with a set of circumstances that are completely out of their control, and yet the companies that employ them continue to use a cookie-cutter approach to help them succeed. In addition, customers are more informed than ever, thanks to all the information at their fingertips online. Almost every buying decision today starts with a Google search, which can make a salesperson's job either much easier or more difficult.

For sales companies to move beyond this current sales environment and allow salespeople to grow and succeed, they must begin to think differently. They must change failed practices and adopt new ideas and creative approaches. After studying many sales training programs, I have found that they focus on a features-and-benefits paradigm or some form of it. They emphasize price, product or performance—or a version of all three—seemingly ignoring that today's customers are primarily looking for value, solutions and peace of mind.

So, how might we think differently about how to develop salespeople? Let me introduce you to Benedict of Nursia.

Meet Benedict the salesman

I was introduced to the Rule of Benedict five years ago, and it profoundly affected me. The tenets of the Rule have led my life since and led me to become a Benedictine Oblate, taking a vow to follow the Rule to the best of my ability. So how does a Monk help you with sales? Benedict of Nursia was born into a noble family in 480 A.D. As a young man, he was sent to study in Rome. He soon witnessed the collapse of the Roman Empire and fled south to the hills of Subiaco to follow the hermit's life. He soon realized that the answer to his personal problems and the problems of the world was to be found not in solitary escape but in laying the foundations of a society based on prayer and work.

In the midst of collapsing institutions, moral decay and social chaos, Benedict established religious communities based on work, prayer and routine. Drawing on earlier monastic writings, Benedict created a very simple document, a "rule" that lays down the principles of monastic life. The *Rule of Saint Benedict* is a classic of Christian spirituality, and the fact that it is still followed by monks and nuns 1,500 years after its composition demonstrates its continued relevance. The rules are not so much a spiritual treatise as a practical guide for living and working in the community. Together, they provide detailed instructions on the monks' liturgical life but also down-to-earth guidelines for the proper qualities of an abbot, prior and cellarer (the leaders of the community.) It outlines how the monks must constantly listen, respect and forgive one another and the attitude they should have toward material things. Benedict's times may not have been much different than the VUCA environment we now operate in. The turmoil and chaos that he experienced we can certainly feel today.

The Rule contained Benedict's thoughts on how his religious community should function, focusing first on pursuing a life in Christ and then showing exactly what that would look like and what was expected. Benedictines are the workers compared to other religious orders. Their motto is *ora et labora*. Work and prayer and life in the monastery has an order to it. Benedict laid out the different movements of the monastery—when monks should pray, when they would work, when they would eat and rest.

The abbot led the monastery, but Benedict believed that all monks, even the young and new ones, should be able to give input on decisions. The tenets of the Rule—obedience, stability, order, hospitality and excellence of everything—were all set forth in the Rule, which would become the primary blueprint for Western civilization long after Benedict was gone. Charlemagne would make the Rule a principle document in institutions, government, schools and even commerce. To this day, the Rule is still the guiding document for many businesses and institutions.

So, why is Benedict relevant to a book on selling? What did Benedict *sell*? He sold an approach to living and working in a community based on work and prayer, *ora et labora.* He sold the promise of salvation based on living by his Rule. Benedict did what Daniel Pink recommended in his book *To Sell is Human*—he moved people from what they thought and believed to a different perspective. We all sell something, but of course, some of us don't sell products and services but rather thoughts and ideas. In doing so, we convince others of new ways of doing things. We move people to change their minds and their behaviors.

The Rule of Benedict is a simple yet demanding way to live and work in community. It presents order but also fairness in how the community is led and how it thrives. Its principles, as you will see in the coming chapters, give us a blueprint of how to achieve excellence in many endeavors, especially in selling.

The Monk Principles©

How might Benedict's Rule help us operate successfully in a sales environment? These rules or principles are what I call the Monk Principles©. There are seven of them, as follows:

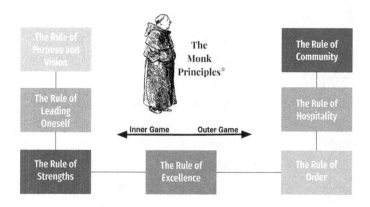

The Rule of Purpose and Vision

This is when we operate not for our own sake but for the sake of a higher purpose. Benedictine monks and nuns live, pray and work for the glory of God as their higher purpose. As salespeople, our higher purpose may be our families, the organizations we support, and maybe if we're lucky, a higher purpose of the company we work for. Vision examines what it means to have vision and how to utilize it daily to achieve our goals. Visualization may be one of the single greatest tools that professional athletes use to achieve success. How, as salespeople, do we use it to do the same?

The Rule of Leading Oneself

Virtue, character and doing the right thing are all ideas we aspire to. They require an understanding of how to develop our character to do the right thing for ourselves, our customers, our company and our families. This is leading oneself. There are many examples of salespeople and organizations going astray in this rule, cutting corners, dishonesty, price gouging, and passing blame. In this rule, we learn to do the right thing *all the time* by utilizing our character strengths. In addition, we come to understand some of the concepts of positive psychology, how to create habits for success and how the pursuit of happiness can help us achieve sales excellence not because of the results we achieve but by excellence in and of itself.

The Rule of Strengths

Achieving the greatest success means that we utilize our God-given talents to the best of our ability. Unfortunately, most sales organizations never let this happen because they shoehorn salespeople into a process that diminishes their talents, not maximizes them. The Rule of Strength examines what our strengths are and how to use them to achieve success.

The Rule of Excellence

Benedictine abbeys have always been self-sustaining, meaning they survive on their own labors. Over the course of 1,500 years, they have always pursued excellence in their labors. It is one of the biggest reasons they make the best beer in the world. The monks believe that if something is worth doing, then it is worth doing to the best of your ability. The Rule of Excellence looks at three specific areas of creating excellence—deep focus, innovative thinking and creating value.

The Rule of Order

The Rule of Order or stability is a key principle. In a monastery or abbey, everything is done in a process—when to eat, when to pray, when to work, how long to sleep—it's all a regimented routine. Of course, in sales, we typically operate by using a process also, but for decades sales organizations have had a cookie-cutter approach to a failed "by the numbers" approach. Regarding this Rule of Order, I'll lay out a different way to use the sales process— one that can be customized to take advantage of each salesperson's unique gifts and talents.

The Rule of Community

Community for Benedictines is the physical monastery or abbey they live in, but the principle of community can be translated to mean anyone we connect with—customers, prospects, vendors and anyone else interested in our work. This idea of community is how we make others feel like they matter, how we value their input, how we listen to their needs, and how we accept their criticism. As salespeople, we find ourselves in many different situations of community. How we operate in these realms can help define our success.

The Rule of Hospitality

Taking care of guests is what the principle of hospitality is all about. We can apply that same principle to creating customer experiences that go beyond traditional customer service. This principle looks at not only providing service but educating customers and creating a process that gets you introduced to others who can use your products and services.

While these principles can stand on their own, Benedict believed it was vital that they be used together. As we apply them to sales, it will be easy to choose one and say, "That one looks good to me." I encourage you, however, to consider that all seven Monk Principles© fit together, and by exercising them all, you will flourish in sales and in life.

In my studies of selling, I've tried to find the edge I could give my clients (salespeople and the organizations they work for) to help them achieve not only success but excellence. I never expected to find that edge in a religious document written over 1,500 years ago by a monk who had documented how to live and work in community in seventy-three short chapters. As I began to pull the principles out of this document and apply them to sales and leadership, I was astounded by how simple they were but equally amazed at how they can dramatically impact the sales profession.

Over the next several chapters, I am going to go through each of these Monk Principles© and show you how to use them to achieve sales success that is also deeply fulfilling. If you are a sales leader reading this book, then strap in because I'm going to challenge the way you've done business and guide you through a process of rethinking how your business or organization can achieve sales success.

The sales hedgehog concept

One of my favorite business books is *Good to Great* by Jim Collins. In the opening line, Collins states, "Good is the enemy of great." Many sales organizations don't change how they develop salespeople because they believe they do it well enough already. I spent nearly twenty-five years working with financial advisors and the firms that employed them, and that industry is notorious for thinking good is good enough. They have been training advisors the same way for fifty years and believe their way is the only way, yet this industry has one of the highest sales failure rates. Over 90 percent of the financial advisors that start in the business won't last two years.

One of the many useful ideas in Collins's book is what he calls the hedgehog concept. It involves three simple components—do what you can be the best at, do what you're passionate about, and do what makes you money. If you are focused on those three things, you have a better chance of achieving success.

THE SALES HEDGEHOG CONCEPT

Passion for what you sell

SALES EXCELLENCE

Use your inner game to be the best you can be

Having systems and support in place and using them

I have a corollary to that concept I call the sales hedgehog concept. It also focuses on three components—have a passion for what you sell, use your inner game to be the best you can be, and have systems and support in place, then use them constantly.

Have a passion for what you sell

It doesn't matter if you sell widgets, houses, financial products or complicated technology, gain a passion for whatever it is you sell. If you don't have it, then find out what true benefits your customers are gaining when they buy and use your products and services. You can't have passion for something that produces no benefits, but understanding the benefits can fuel your passion.

When I started working in the life insurance industry, my father told me I wouldn't truly have a passion for what I was selling until I delivered my first death claim check. Sure enough, I delivered that first check to a friend whose business partner had died and saw what it meant to him. It meant he could keep the business going without financial strain. So, if you don't have a passion for what you sell, develop a passion or go sell something else.

Use your inner game to be the best you can be

I will talk more about the inner game later, but if you aren't using that space between your ears to be the best you can be, you will never find sales excellence. As a former professional golfer, I understand that the most important real estate on the golf course doesn't have grass on it. It's the space between your ears. I've seen countless talented golf professionals who didn't make it because they didn't understand the inner game. I was one of them and only wish I might have discovered this secret much earlier (although I couldn't putt either.)

Constantly use your systems and support mechanisms

Consider this third component of the sales hedgehog concept as the *outer* game of selling. It's all about finding what works and then replicating it time and time again. I remember being on the golf course with Gary Player and watching him hit a three-iron exactly 210 yards into a circle about six feet in diameter. When I asked how he could do that so consistently, he answered, "I've practiced that exact swing thousands of times so it's become automatic. When I get in the heat of battle, I don't have to worry about the mechanics of my swing. I can focus on the changing conditions of the shot and the course." Pretty good advice for golf, sales or anything else.

If we can combine all three of these components from the sales hedgehog concept and practice them diligently, we can create sales excellence. But the effort cannot only be made by the individual salespeople. The sales organization and sales managers must give each salesperson the help and support they need. Unfortunately, as I mentioned earlier, sales managers and organizations are sometimes the biggest hurdles. We will discuss this in detail later.

Questions to ask yourself

1. What are the things holding me back from sales flourishing?

2. What Monk Principles© resonate with me and why?

3. How am I using the Sales Hedgehog Concept to excel?

Chapter 2
Sales Training vs. Sales Development–
The Inner Work of Selling

Many sales organizations have spent countless millions of dollars on programs to train their sales teams. And many sales training companies and individuals have made countless millions providing these programs. These programs go back to the early days of sales training, which were primarily geared toward motivation, and then, with programs developed by Xerox and IBM, focused on the technical side of sales training. These programs evolved into courses aimed at specific industries.

Later, sales training programs began to delve into the intellectual aspect of selling, which sprung from books like *Conceptual Selling* and *Strategic*

Selling. From Dale Carnegie, Napoleon Hill and Zig Ziglar to countless other sales "gurus," sales trainers have promised to help teams find that magic bullet that would take them to the next level.

The focus of sales training

Sales training has primarily been focused on four core areas:

- Selling skills
- Product training
- Company-specific training
- Motivation

According to the American Society of Training and Development (ASTD), these topics account for virtually 95 percent of all sales training done in organizations. Selling skills account for one-third of that training, with product training a close second. The most popular method for delivering this training is classroom instruction, and the least popular is coaching and in-field support.

In another study, it was reported that US businesses spend $15 billion per year on sales training and an average of $2,000 per salesperson. Unfortunately, most of the salespeople trained believed the training was ineffective or less than useful. A primary reason they found it ineffective was the training did not get top-down support from higher-level management. Thus it was not carried forward into the field and implemented within their sales plans. Most of the training turned out to be a reactive approach to competitive markets and was focused on the sales transaction.

Person-centric, strengths-based selling

Selling is a noble profession, yet in many cases, salespeople are viewed in a negative light. They are depicted as pushy, aggressive, dishonest, sneaky and lacking integrity. How salespeople react to these perceptions ultimately will determine their success. Most sales training and development focuses on improving tactics and strategies to overcome these negative perceptions or attempting to motivate the sales team to keep going despite the negative perceptions. There is a better way to address these perceptions, one that focuses instead on the individuality of the salesperson. It emphasizes using the individual's unique, God-given talents and strengths. I call this approach person-centric, strengths-based selling.

Unfortunately, many salespeople have been their own worst enemies because of the manipulative methods they use. Organizations have encouraged these methods by training them and managing expectations based on false assumptions.

One of my favorite movies is *Glengarry Glenn Ross*, about real estate salespeople. In the movie,

David Mamet introduces us to the pressures and machinations of salespeople in real estate, which is a microcosm of the reality of the USA. He presents a world in which the sales team is dominated by the need to close their leads; otherwise, they would lose their jobs. This is a world of corrupt values where people are prepared to mislead and manipulate others to help themselves. The love of money by the salespeople is so great that they become selfish, devious, materialistic and extremely competitive. In this pressurized environment, if you close the sales (ABC - Always Be Closing), you win. The movie's portrayal of salespeople is all too familiar in sales organizations today. There is a better way, and it starts with redefining sales.

For most people, selling is providing goods and/or services for the exchange of money. But this is a very simplistic view. *A more useful definition is that selling is the exchange of ideas and concepts that move people to understand new ways of looking at things, accepting solutions to problems, taking care of basic needs and making people feel better.*

Just about any product or service can fit within this revised description, but the main point is that selling is about people. It's about the exchange of ideas and concepts to get people to think about their problems, circumstances or wants and needs and then providing a solution to address that.

If we start with people in the selling equation, it reframes the whole process. And if we recognize the salesperson as a human being—not a programmable robot—then it should also reframe the whole process of training and developing salespeople.

The sales development process starts on the inside, or what I call the inner game of selling. Working with sales teams to help them understand who they are personally—what their character strengths and work talents are—gives each salesperson the foundation to take those strengths and apply them to the sales process as best suits them. This is a very different approach than most sales organizations take.

Most organizations start with the sales process and then "fit" salespeople into the process without regard for each person's strengths and talents. Attempting to "clone" the best salespeople is how many organizations build the process. But I've worked with hundreds of high-producing salespeople, and none of them sell the same way. They all have different methods and mindsets they have perfected through practice and self-discipline.

Once a salesperson understands their inner game, that person must learn to develop habits of excellence. This is where The Rule of Excellence fits in—helping salespeople understand which approaches to focus on, innovation, and creating value.

Once you have taken the first two steps in the development ladder below, it is time to define the process, which is based on each salesperson's inner game and habits of excellence. Each person's process may be a little different depending on their specific strengths. The process that I will lay out in the Rule of Order (covered later) takes a step-by-step approach but is flexible enough to be customized by each salesperson so that it fits their strengths. The process is a combination of prospecting, educating, listening, understanding and providing solutions, then continues through the delivery and follow-up.

INTERIOR WORK OF SELLING

DEVELOPING HABITS OF EXCELLENCE

CONCEPTUAL SALES PROCESS

COACHING

SALES FLOURISHING

The last step in sales development is coaching and mentoring. Unfortunately, this is where many sales organizations fail because they only provide sales *management*, and that management is driven by numbers and results. By providing salespeople with a coach and/or mentor, the sales organizations can have someone to accompany each salesperson through the development work, and that coach can help them become the salespersons they aspire to be.

The inner game of selling

The Interior Work of Selling

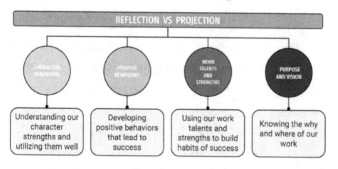

Most sales training programs start with exterior tactical work—how to prospect, present, overcome objections and offer products and services with a focus on features and benefits. However, if we start by focusing on the need to develop people from the inside first, this opens up a whole new possibility for creating successful salespeople.

Interior work focuses on self-reflection and how each salesperson understands their own strengths and talents, how they create positive behaviors, and how they persevere through the highs and lows of selling. In her book, *St.*

Benedict's Toolbox, Jane Tomaine talks about this inner work that Benedict refers to in the Rule. It's called conversatio. She says,

> Conversatio has an outward aspect—a change of behavior and attitude—as well as an inner meaning-transformation in the heart where we actually become a different person, a different kind of being.

Over the years, I have seen great results from putting these ideas and concepts to work. The interior work of selling begins with the idea of character—what Alexander Havard, author of *The Virtuous Leader*, calls the "content of character." According to Havard:

> It is virtue, or more precisely the set of classical human virtues—above all, magnanimity, humility, prudence, courage, self-control and justice.

These same virtues apply to salespeople. Virtues that are not intrinsic to a particular human being can be developed by habits over time. This isn't a new concept. In Stephen Covey's book *The Seven Habits of Highly Effective People*, the author describes his study of success literature in the US since 1776. Here is what he found:

> The success literature for the past fifty years was superficial, filled with techniques and

quick fixes with social Band-Aids and aspirin. In stark contrast, almost all of the literature in the first 150 years or so focused on what could be called the Character Ethic as the foundation of success-things like integrity, humility, simplicity, modesty and the Golden Rule. Thus, in a little over a generation we have largely abandoned the enduring character qualities that shaped our history.

Covey believed that if we focused first on this inside-out approach starting with the Character Ethic, we would understand that improving ourselves on the inside leads to success on the outside.

So, what are these sales virtues mentioned by Havard, and why are they important to salespeople? Here are the key virtues and what they can do for a salesperson:

- **Courage** to stay the course and resist pressures of all kinds.
- **Temperance** to maintain focus on the mission at hand and avoid distractions of all sorts.
- **Wisdom** to learn and use an increasing base of knowledge to do the right thing.
- **Magnanimity** to strive for great things, to challenge yourself and others.
- **Humility** to be a humble servant and overcome selfishness so you can better serve others.

Building virtues into sales development takes longer to accomplish, of course. The organization must exercise radical patience in developing salespeople, coaching and nurturing them, but the results often are more engaged, and loyal salespeople who become successful for the right reasons and always put first the mission and purpose of the organization and the relationship of the customer. Salespeople are developed to make conscious decisions based on how they impact the customer and the company first and their sales income second. This becomes a win for the organization, the customer and long-term for each salesperson.

There are many examples of companies that got this order wrong. One of the most recent is Wells Fargo, which put the sale of their products above their relationships with their customers and expected their salespeople to push products that were neither needed nor ethically of value to their customers. The mass cross-selling scheme cost the bank millions in fines and billions in lost assets, but more importantly, they lost the trust of their customers. It will take a long time to get that back.

When it comes to the interior work of selling, we must look at the strengths and talents of each salesperson and align them with how they sell. Most sales organizations completely miss this because they believe they can simply clone their best salespeople to repeat the successful methods of their top sellers.

I can remember working with a client who had hired a salesperson that was making great progress but wasn't meeting company expectations for following the prescribed process. It didn't matter that his overall sales results were ahead of where he should have been. He was using his own strengths to build sales and didn't need to make as many sales calls as some of the other salespeople in the organization. He was also very successful in closing sales. The sales manager believed this salesperson wasn't doing his best because his prescribed activity level in various tactics was lower than others. This sales manager was confusing activity with accomplishment. The salesperson's true accomplishments were obtained by doing those things his customers wanted him to do but doing it in his own way.

To work on your strengths and talents you must understand them and how they apply to the selling environment. For over twenty years, I've used the Clifton StrengthsFinder to assess a salesperson's strengths and help them determine the best way to use their strengths in selling. Admittedly, this flies in the face of the way most sales organizations assume there are only certain strengths that fit with being a successful salesperson. I can affirm, however, that in working with hundreds of salespeople using the

Clifton tool, I have seen salespeople succeed with many different combinations of strengths that Clifton assesses. I'll delve more deeply into this area in the Rule of Strengths and Talents.

Positive Sales Behaviors

Over the years, speakers and authors like Dale Carnegie, Napoleon Hill and Zig Ziglar have espoused the benefits of a positive attitude and positive thinking. I have been a big fan of their work and believe that their influence has helped many. But positive psychology goes much deeper into the science of positive *behaviors*, and in the selling profession, there is nothing more important than positive behaviors.

The science of positive psychology has only been around since the late 1990s when Dr. Martin Seligman proclaimed in a speech that it was time for the practice of psychology to stop focusing on taking someone with psychosis or addictions (assigned a -10) and trying to get them to normal (0). Seligman suggested working on getting people who were normal (0) and developing them to flourishing (+10).

Until that time, psychology was focused almost entirely on helping abnormalities. What Seligman and many of his colleagues began to focus on was, were the key components of happiness and how can people achieve it?

Positive psychology and positive behaviors are rarely talked about in sales, but they represent a big factor in sales success. When positive behaviors are put to work, they help create positive deviance that significantly exceeds the norm, which is exactly what most salespeople and organizations want to do. The positive behaviors that we will concentrate on are:

- **Gratitude**: Being grateful for what you have—your success, your customers, your work, and all the interactions that you have with people.

- **Empathy**: Showing compassion, understanding and compassion in your dealings with others; putting their situation ahead of yours.

- **Hope**: Having a positive outlook that enables you to self-motivate, set goals and be flexible when things change.

- **Active Listening**: Not just hearing what others say but actively listening to understand what is being said.

- **Efficacy**: Having confidence in who you are and what you want to achieve and knowing that you are capable of achieving it in the right way.

- **Optimism**: Having a positive mental attitude that always looks at the upside, which allows you to overcome even the most difficult times.

- **Grit**: Grit and perseverance are how the tough get going when the going gets tough; the ability to keep your head down and keep plugging away even when things are rough.

We'll cover all these positive behaviors in the chapter on the Rule of Leading Oneself.

Purpose and Vision

The last inner game concept is purpose and vision. In order to achieve sales excellence, it is vital to know why you do what you do and where you want to go. By connecting our "why" of sales to our vision of where we want to go, we create something beyond simply sales results. Most sales organizations measure success by numbers or results, and you're only considered successful if you hit certain results-driven benchmarks.

But what about salespeople who aren't the top performer but are consistently in the top quartile and move about their work creating sales and building a loyal following of customers? Many of these only work hard because they commit their time also to their families and relationships. Are we to assume they aren't successful and aren't a benefit to the organization? Give me a team of those salespeople versus the hyper-successful workaholics because their priorities are in the right place. They are dedicated to doing the right thing and committed to a vision of a higher purpose.

The next three chapters will focus on the inner game Rules. We will go into detail about what they are, how they work and how to use them effectively. Then we'll transition from the inner game to the outer game with the Rule of Excellence. From there, the next three chapters will move into the outer game or projection, the Rules that focus on interacting with others and the tools for doing that effectively.

Questions to ask yourself

1. What parts of the inner game of selling do I need to work on the most?

2. Which positive behaviors am I most interested in being better at?

3. How does the sales development model differ from other training I've received?

Chapter 3
The Rule of Purpose and Vision

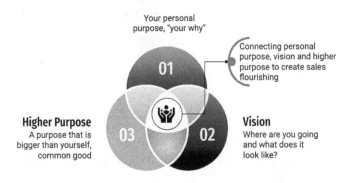

Your personal purpose, "your why"

01

Connecting personal purpose, vision and higher purpose to create sales flourishing

Higher Purpose
A purpose that is bigger than yourself, common good

03

02

Vision
Where are you going and what does it look like?

Benedict is very clear in his purpose as he lays out his rule. He teaches the monks what the purpose is in the first lines of the Rule,

> …then if you are ready to give up your own will, once and for all, and armed with the strong and noble weapons of obedience to do battle for the true King, Christ the Lord (P:3).

When purpose is clear, great things can happen. Studies show that when we think about our impact on others or directly help someone else, we get a boost of the "happiness trifecta" of neurotransmitters—oxytocin, dopamine and serotonin. Oxytocin supports empathy and social bonding. Dopamine plays a major role in motivation and movement. Serotonin regulates mood. The results are desirable outcomes like increased engagement, motivation and a sense of fulfillment.

As a motivator, purpose lasts longer than achievements or results. Results *push* people for the short-term, but a bigger other-centered purpose *pulls* them for the long term. This is partly why Angela Duckworth, professor of psychology at the University of Pennsylvania and bestselling author of *Grit*, found in her comprehensive study on resilience that the pulling force of purpose is one of the key predictors of grit. "Grit," Duckworth said, "is stamina, but it's not just stamina in your effort. It's also stamina in your direction."

Cultivating a motivated, fulfilled, engaged and gritty workforce starts with purpose. Gallup surveys show that the primary motivator for fulfilling work is finding and connecting meaning and purpose to our work. So what is *purpose*?

Simon Sinek, author of the book *Start With Why*, said in his TEDX talk "The Golden Circle" that most people easily identify what they do and some identify how they do it, but they miss the most crucial aspect—*why* they do what they do.

On November 19, 1863, a large crowd gathered to hear speakers give homage to a valiant effort. Edward Everett, one of the great orators of his time, had been slated to give a two-hour "Gettysburg address" that day. Following him was President Abraham Lincoln. Everett's oration, now nearly forgotten, was nearly 14,000 words long. Lincoln, however, in just 271 words and taking less than two minutes to deliver, became the speech known today as the Gettysburg Address and is one of the most well-known speeches in US history. In his speech, Lincoln defined the purpose of the American Civil War in these powerful words:

...that these dead shall not have died in vain— that this nation, under God, shall have a new birth of freedom and that government of the people, by the people, for the people, shall not perish from the earth.

With those words, Lincoln clearly defined what the North needed to do. Arguably, this speech turned the tide of the war and led to the North's ultimate victory.

The Purpose mindset

Our mindset has a direct relationship to our purpose. Zach Mercurio, author of *The Invisible Leader*, talks about this mindset. His favorite question, which he frequently asks those he encounters, is, "how have you changed the world today?" Mercurio says that he gets a variety of responses to that question but, in most cases, gets only silence. Most people don't feel like they matter enough to change the world, and yet every one of us has the ability to do something, however small, that can change the world of those we know. About the belief that no individual can affect others in meaningful ways, Mercurio goes on to say:

This type of thinking is a trap. Every person, in any organization, changes the world whether we acknowledge it or not. Acknowledging our capacity is the first step toward developing a purposeful mindset. I think the false idea that we can't create big change in small, everyday ways stems from the dominant conceptualizations of leadership... When we define impact in such limited terms, we disinvite nearly everyone from changing the world, even though they change it everyday.

Types of purpose

There are two types of purpose—personal purpose and higher purpose. Personal purpose is why we get out of bed in the morning, what motivates us to do what we do, and why we work in the jobs we have. A recent Gallup study found that 68 percent of people who are not satisfied at work are also not satisfied with their lives. Conversely, 79 percent of those who are satisfied at work are likewise satisfied with their lives.

In understanding our personal purpose, we must look backward, not forward. Many think that finding purpose means looking to the future to see what we might be. But instead, it starts with where we were and why we got to where we are now—what led us to get into selling or moving people in the first place. We can't define our personal purpose until we understand the answers to those questions.

In Sinek's book, *Start With Why*, he points out:

We must first answer the question, why do I get out of bed in the morning and why should anyone care? Does our personal purpose give us something we can commit to?

Personal Purpose – Why do you sell what you sell?

Purpose starts with personal purpose, understanding why you do what you do. This has nothing to do with what you sell or what your company's purpose is. It is a more personal connection. What gets you out of bed in the morning to go to work selling something? In his book *As a Man Thinketh*, James Allen writes:

Until thought is linked with purpose, there is no intelligent accomplishment.

Connecting purpose with your work in sales gives you meaning. Connecting that meaning to your work creates excellence.

What led you to sales? Was it because you enjoyed working with people? Was it because you loved helping people? Did you have a passion for your industry or product or service? Maybe you wanted to be with the company you're affiliated with. Whatever the reason, the answer to this question can help you identify your purpose.

Purpose also helps create the positive behavior of perseverance, which I'll talk more about in the next chapter. I can remember from an early age watching my father in sales and understanding he was really helping people, and so I felt called to do something to help people too. That purpose has taken me down a variety of different paths, including teaching and discerning the priesthood, but ultimately it led to my work over the last thirty years.

Looking back, though, I now understand that when my focus has been about money, attaining success and acquiring possessions, I have not done nearly so well and have not been happy in my work. Purpose is what gets me out of bed in the morning.

Vocation and purpose

What is a vocation? It's much more than just a job—it's a calling, a connection to what you were meant to do. Interestingly, most people don't think of sales as a calling. Rarely do I hear someone say they've wanted to be a salesperson since they were a kid. Generally, they think of selling in another way—like helping people, providing solutions and making people happy. In many cases, the vocation of selling is about helping people. If you look at the most successful salespeople, most of them have a calling to help others.

If we think of our work, how does it compare to the parable of the bricklayers? It goes like this. There were three bricklayers building a church. When the first one was asked about his work, he said his job was laying bricks. The second bricklayer said his job was to build a church. The third bricklayer, however, said he was building the house of God.

When you think about your selling profession, do you see it as a job, a career or a calling? Those that identify their work as a calling are more passionate about what they sell, and usually, they are happier and more successful than others.

Higher purpose

Higher purpose means connecting your work to something higher than yourself. When you connect your sales to a higher purpose, you're moving from a job to a calling. Higher purpose always looks outward, which means you are doing something beyond yourself and for something that is greater for others. Robert Quinn, a professor at the Ross School of Business at the University of Michigan and author of *The Economics of Higher Purpose*, defines higher purpose as:

An organization of higher purpose is a social system in which the greater good has been envisioned, articulated and authenticated. Like all organizations, an organization of higher purpose is a cauldron of conflict. Yet the higher purpose is the arbiter of all decisions, and people find meaning in their work and in their relationships despite the conflicts. They share a vision and are fully engaged. They strive to transcend their egos and sacrifice for the common good.... Higher purpose is the prosocial

> goal that is defined not in terms of economic
> output but in terms of contribution to society.

So, when Starbucks states that its reason for being is to provide its customers "a third place between work and home," it is articulating a higher purpose that transcends its business goals yet intersects with them.

The higher purpose of some companies is clear. A fraternal insurance company probably has a higher purpose of supporting whatever religion or organization to which they are aligned. The higher purpose of other companies may be to help people or the environment or to address some other societal issue. If you work for one of these types of companies, connecting your purpose to the organization's higher purpose should be quite simple, yet I have seen salespeople who work for such companies become focused on their own success and income rather than the higher purpose of the company. These salespeople typically don't last long. If they are not outwardly focused but are solely worried about making money and paying bills, it's difficult to focus on a higher purpose.

In Ron Willinghams' book, *The Inner Game of Selling,* the author writes:

> A survival focus can force us into its small
> emotional prison cell, making us fight like

crazy to get out. But it's in the fight that we can gain the strength of character to move forward. The will to fight through our struggles is fueled by the strength of our purpose.

Vision

The last aspect of the Rule of Vision and Purpose is vision, which is about where you want to go.

I ran my first marathon back in 2001. As I signed up for the race, I realized that I had no experience or training to run a marathon. I also knew that for my name to show up in the paper as an official marathon finisher, I had to complete the race in under six hours. I immediately created a vision of crossing the finish line with the clock registering under six hours. We often hear athletes talk about "visualization" and creating an image in their minds of what a desired result will look like.

In the movie *7 Days in Utopia*, Robert Duvall plays a wise, old sage and former golf pro who gets Luke, his protégé, to paint a picture of the shot he wants to make. This is vision! In my office hangs a picture of me crossing the finish line in my first marathon in five hours and fifty-four minutes. I made the paper!

Two kinds of vision: inward and outward

There are two kinds of vision, inward-looking and outward-looking. Inward-looking vision requires us to address our current reality. Here is an example. I may want to be a point guard in the NBA, but I also know that the current reality is that I'm sixty-four years old and have a vertical jump of about one foot. Most likely, I am not going to fit as a point guard in the NBA, no matter how much my vision wants me to. Therefore, we have to understand the current reality and then create an outward vision based on our inward-looking vision of that reality. Inward-looking is kind of like using a microscope, whereas outward-looking vision uses a telescope.

The outward-looking vision we create requires three components. First, it must have a picture of where we want to go—in other words, what we want to achieve. The second component is a road map that shows how we are going to get there. What do we need to do for that vision to be achieved? Finally, the outward-looking vision must help us understand what it's going to look like when we achieve our vision. Think about it from an emotional standpoint of how it will feel, taste and appear.

Let's start with goals

Every business and sales organization has goals. Some are broad goals, and some are very specific goals that are broken down into minutia and measured incessantly. In Marcus Buckingham and Ashely Goodall's book *Nine Lies About Work* they talk about goals:

> Leaders set quotas because they want to stimulate the performance of their salespeople. But quotas don't work like that. The very best salespeople hit their quota months before the end of the year, whereupon they do the sales equivalent of vanishing off home—that is, they start to delay the closing of their deals so that they can "bank" them and ensure that they begin next year with a head start. Sales goals actually degrade the performance of their top salespeople.
>
> But what about salespeople who are struggling or middle of the road? Won't goals serve to stretch them upward toward their quota, in much the same way a friend's marathon goal will help stretch toward greater endurance? Well, again, not exactly. In reality, what happens to middling or struggling salespeople is that their imposed quota increases pressure on them. And this is not a self-imposed pressure that comes from attempting to achieve some-

thing we feel is important. Now this pressure to achieve company-imposed goals is coercion, and coercion is a cousin to fear. In the worst cases, fear-fueled employees push and push and, falling short, resort to sometimes illegal tactics to meet their goals.

This is exactly what happened with Wells Fargo, which I mentioned earlier.

Vision versus goals

Most people set goals they want to achieve, and almost all sales organizations require their salespeople to have goals. As Buckingham says in the quotation above, there is one big problem with goal-setting. The minute it becomes apparent that the goals will be achieved, we go into coast mode.

In my many years of working with salespeople, I have observed this phenomenon repeatedly. Salespeople reach their annual goals in September and then basically coast through the last three months of the year. Or, if a salesperson discovers that they won't achieve their goals at all, they begin to make excuses. You've heard them, I'm sure. "The market conditions weren't right." "I lost my best customer." "A big deal suddenly fell through."

We all know that few sales organizations are going to stop goal setting, but there is a way for individual salespeople to achieve goals in a more positive way by creating a vision of what life will look like when they reach their goals. My wife and I create a vision board at the beginning of every year. It includes some goals but also incorporates images of what we want to achieve. We have been doing this for many years… with a few exceptions. And when I haven't done it, hitting my goals has been much more challenging. Just as athletes visualize what they want to see happen, salespeople can also create their own images of the results they want to achieve.

In creating this vision, take into consideration three things. First, visualize the endpoint—what will it look like? Second, what will the *journey* look like—imagine some of the images of that journey. Lastly, what will the *results or accomplishments* look like? Visualize the completion of the vision.

I recently built a new patio, and we put it on our vision board. The first step of the vision was understanding what the patio would look like—drawing it out and creating a picture of it. Then we figured out what it would take to build it—the materials, the excavation, the laying of the pavers, et cetera. Finally, we imagined the project completed and some of the benefits—dinners and parties with family and friends, all of us enjoying the new patio space.

Impact: Combining higher purpose and vision

When you combine the power of higher purpose with a vision, you bring together two of the most powerful aspects of achievement. This starts with what I call the higher-purpose question. That question is simply, "How can I help?" When we ask that simple question, we move from focusing on *ourselves* to focusing on something greater than ourselves. This question has led to some of the greatest successes in business, education, healthcare and institutions. The answer to that question could be a focus on our families, our friends, a cause that we support, or the common good. It becomes especially powerful when we combine it with a vision of what that will look like, how it will feel to help, and the reaction of those you're helping. One of my favorite quotes is from G. K. Chesterton:

> How much larger your life would be if you could become smaller in it; if you could look at others with common curiosity and pleasure [...]. You would break out of this tiny and tawdry theater in which your own little plot is always being played, and you would find yourself under a freer sky, in a street full of splendid strangers.

Combining higher purpose and vision allows us to find that freer sky and move out of our own goals and accomplishments to that street full of splendid strangers and the world around us. When that becomes our focus and the reason for doing what we do, we move from success to impact.

The Rule of Purpose and Vision is about understanding why you do what you do and where you want to go while maintaining focus on something more than yourself.

Questions to ask yourself

1. Why do I sell what I sell?

2. How can I connect my work with a higher purpose, something beyond myself? What is the answer to "How can I help?"

3. What does my vision of what I want to accomplish look like over the next year, two years and five years? (Be specific: how does that vision look, what does the journey feel like, and how do you feel when the results are accomplished?

Chapter 4
The Rule of Leading Oneself

Benedict begins the fourth chapter of the Rule talking about "tools for good works." These tools are the building blocks for being a good monk. Of these tools, he concludes at the end of the chapter:

> …these then are the tools of the spiritual craft. When we have used them without ceasing day and night and have returned them on judgment day, our wages will be the reward the Lord has promised." (RB 4: 75–77)

As you study these tools, you will likely agree that these are also tools for living well, essential tools for being a good person—and a good salesperson. Wouldn't you agree that the following "tools" fit both of those categories?

- Don't act in anger.
- Don't be deceitful.
- Don't grumble.
- Don't be lazy.
- Be humble.
- Guide your tongue from evil.
- Don't be jealous.
- Respect others.

All of these "tools" provide sound advice for good living and good selling. Benedict's Rule has many chapters about how to be a good monk, and this self-work also applies to the inner game of selling. I think we can all look over every item on this list and say, "I could have done *that* better or differently."

The Rule of Leading Oneself is about self-inspection that applies not only to selling well but living good lives, the pursuit of virtues, and using our character strengths to do the right things. Benedict believed that living and working in community was also about living and exercising virtue.

Positive psychology

Positive psychology is known as the science of virtue and flourishing. But before I get into that, I want to touch on an important difference between personality and character because it's an important distinction. There are many types of personality assessment systems, such as DISC, Myer-Briggs and Enneagram. These personality inventories help us understand how we're hardwired to think and respond to the environment in different ways and how we can be our best selves based on that hardwiring.

Many sales organizations use personality assessments such as the Sales Achievement Predictor and Caliper to determine whether someone will achieve success in sales. The problem is that while these tools assess personality types, they do not assess character, which is different. Character is something developed by habits, which we will talk more about later. Character can be impacted by our environments and created by our experiences and how we choose to face them. Character strengths/traits are virtues in action. These character strengths have only recently been studied in the science of positive psychology. We know from these studies that leaders are not born, they are built.

The term positive psychology was first used in 2000 by Dr. Martin Seligman in an address to the American Psychological Association. In his talk, he discussed the concept that until then, psychology had mainly studied getting people with problems to a "normal" state. However, there had been no studies on getting "normal" people to live better, more flourishing lives.

Traditionally, psychology had focused on the treatment of problems—for example, people with depression, addiction or psychosis—and getting them from a negative five to zero. Seligman believed there should be another part of science that is aimed at taking a normal person and giving them the tools to flourish and be happy. This concept started the movement. Since then, positive psychology has become a huge area of study.

Virtue and character in sales

Character refers to those aspects of personality that are morally valued. Character strengths are defined as a family of widely valued positive traits tied to virtue and reflected in thoughts, feelings and behaviors. These character strengths exist in degrees and can be measured as individual differences. Character strengths are the psychological ingredients – processes or mechanisms—that define the virtues.

Said another way, character strengths are distinguishable routes to displaying one or another of the virtues. For example, the virtue of wisdom can be achieved through such strengths as creativity, curiosity, love of learning, open-mindedness and what we call perspective—having a big picture of life.

How do we measure character? The classification of character strengths and virtues was developed by Seligman and Chris Peterson, who began by listing virtues and character strengths that could be measured. Character has been studied for thousands of years by philosophers like Aristotle and Confucius to theologians like St. Thomas Aquinas.

Seligman and Peterson developed their Values in Action Inventory (VIA) in 2004. It focuses on what is right about people—specifically, the character strengths that make a good life possible. The VIA has six categories built around virtues. The virtues and related character strengths have a commonality across many different philosophies; in other words, the six virtues they selected show up in some form across various cultures and regions.

Notable character strengths are called signature strengths. These are positive traits that a person owns, celebrates and exercises frequently. Seligman and Peterson identified twenty-four character strengths and created the VIA as a way to measure these strengths in people. The VIA has been taken by over fifteen million people, so it has a rich data set on which to base findings. It's important to note that the VIA assesses strengths, and there are twenty-four identified strengths. A person's twenty-fourth strength is not a weakness, however—just one that you don't use naturally but is still a strength. You can take the Values in Action Inventory here: https://principledflourishing.pro.viasurvey.org/.

The Sales Virtues

The sales virtues are like the virtues that Seligman came up with, but they are more focused on how we relate to others in selling. The five sales virtues are those that I believe are most important and the ones I see exercised most by salespeople.

Courage

Courage in selling is an important virtue. Having courage to make the next call, deliver the presentation and sometimes deliver bad news is important in the sales role. But when we take a deeper look at the virtue of courage as it relates to selling, we find that courage also means doing the morally right thing in the face of difficulty. It means we are always honest and open to taking calculated risks. Most importantly, it means we persevere even in difficult times. The VIA character strengths that relate to the virtue of courage are:

- Bravery
- Perseverance
- Honest
- Zest

Wisdom

Wisdom in selling isn't just about what we know but about making the right decisions, facing reality and being honest with yourself. Wisdom also helps us weigh the facts before making a decision. When we're not certain about something, wisdom leads to asking for help and advice. Wisdom is also the virtue that helps us learn what we need to make our work more successful. The VIA character strengths associated with wisdom are:

- Creativity
- Curiosity
- Judgment
- Love of learning
- Perspective

Temperance

Self-control defines temperance. It's putting to work your good passions and controlling your bad passions. I can remember briefly working in the liquor business in college and watching the sales reps in that industry, which, of course, often fell into alcoholism. I could see those reps that were struggling with the idea of temperance or self-control and those who were able to control the urges and opportunities to have a cocktail—maybe a few—with clients. The VIA character strengths that fall under temperance are:

- Forgiveness
- Self-regulation
- Prudence
- Fairness

Humility

Humility is one of the greatest and most important sales virtues. Humility is all about service to others. It requires an awareness of ourselves and our personal abilities. It's also an awareness of the shortcomings of others and still treating them with dignity. It's a realistic understanding of our own talents and even our lack of talents. Humble salespersons are all about serving and helping others succeed. The VIA Character Strengths for humility are:

- Humility
- Gratitude
- Humor

- Teamwork
- Spirituality

Magnanimity

The last sales virtue is magnanimity, a term that most of us are not familiar with but an important sales virtue because it puts the solutions and success of our customers/clients/prospects first. Magnanimity is the desire for greatness in those we serve. It's about bringing out the greatness in others while moving toward great things for ourselves. It requires an awareness of our own strengths, behaviors, talents and dignity. Magnanimity is about being the best we can be for the people we serve so that they can be the best they can be. The VIA character strengths for magnanimity are:

- Love
- Kindness
- Social intelligence
- Hope
- Leadership
- Appreciation for beauty

Understanding the sales virtues and how your character strengths match up with them is vital as you begin to use your top character strengths as a means of pursuing sales excellence. In Ryan Niemiec's book *The Power of Character Strengths,* he explains why character strengths matter.

> Let's examine this question from two perspectives…. When things are going well, we can use character strengths to help us see what is best in ourselves and others. When things are going poorly, we can use character strengths to give balance to life's struggles we face, to shift the focus from the negative to the positive, to avoid becoming overly self-critical thinking about our strengths rather than what's wrong with us. Enacting the character strengths, our awe for beauty and excellence, or our curiosity can help us notice the good things around us, discover how we can do better and catalyze positive, virtuous, healthy, or more balanced behavior.

When we understand our character strengths and the virtues they accompany and we put them to work in balance, we begin to live our best lives, and through that, we allow others to live their best lives. This ability gives us superpowers when it comes to sales. It gives us the tools to not only elevate ourselves but to elevate others as well—customers, colleagues, or family and friends.

To find out what your character strengths are, go to: https://principledflourishing.pro.viasurvey.org/.

There you can take the VIA for free and find out what your top character strengths are. Click the link to print out the full report and you will see the ranking of your twenty-four-character strengths.

Positive Sales Behaviors

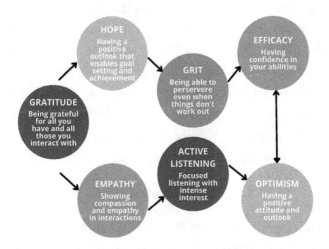

Positive psychology, as we have learned, is the study of happiness. So, let me ask if you would rather buy something from a happy person or a miserable person? Happy salespeople are successful salespeople. There are specific behaviors that, when exercised, connect to the sales virtues. These behaviors give the salesperson a big advantage over someone who does not exhibit those behaviors, and they can lead a salesperson to dramatically outperform the norm. Here are the seven positive sales behaviors:

MIKE FERRELL

Gratitude

Gratitude is being thankful for all we receive. This behavior has incredible benefits, including a longer life, a lower risk of heart disease and reduced or eliminated mental illness. It also does amazing things for sales performance. Spending just five minutes a day on a simple gratitude exercise can pay enormous rewards. Such an exercise can be simply writing down three things you're grateful for at the end of each day—and they don't have to be big things. Your list could include having a good cup of coffee or finding a prime parking space. Creating a habit out of this and doing it daily can reap huge rewards. This is the first step to finding happiness.

Active Listening

The opening line of the Rule says we should listen with the ear of our hearts, meaning we should actively listen with empathy and compassion, trying to understand the person who is talking. Active listening also requires effective questioning, understanding what questions need to be asked and then having the skill to ask them effectively. In Jim Collins's book *Good to Great*, he writes that his favorite opening question is to ask someone where they are from. This question can take several different directions, of course. By using active listening, we can begin to find common ground, which

66

I will talk about later. Active listening is also a little like drinking a fine wine. You don't just pop the cork and drink it—you let it breathe first to build the flavors. Active listening requires us to pause before responding immediately, letting our answer develop more fully before we speak.

Grit/Perseverance

In her book *Grit*, Angela Duckworth writes:

> No matter what the domain, the highly successful had a kind of ferocious determination that played out in two ways: First, these exemplars were unusually resilient and hardworking. Second, they knew in a very, very deep way what it was they wanted. They not only had determination, they had direction.

Duckworth's formula is

talent x effort = skill

When you take your acquired skills and use them, you follow her second formula,

skill x effort = achievement

According to Duckworth, then, even genius doesn't count a lot unless you work hard to improve and use your natural or acquired gifts. What matters most, she suggests, is continual effort. You must persevere when you experience setbacks or disappointments, especially when, by your own standards, you are successful.

Life demands nonstop effort, which both requires and nourishes grit. You need grit to keep going. Keeping at it grants you more grit. We all know that perseverance has always been an important part of sales, especially in the face of rejection, but grit also applies to the inner game, which requires that we continue to put forth the effort to work on ourselves and our inner skills, including character strengths and talents. Grit is the combination of passion and purpose.

Compassion and Empathy

Doing something good for someone without expecting anything in return does amazing things for our mental health. By showing compassion and empathy, we focus on someone else and not ourselves. It is one of the key ingredients of happiness.

Hope

Hope is an optimistic state of mind based on an expectation of positive outcomes. As a verb, it means to "expect with confidence" and to "cherish a desire with anticipation."

Efficacy

Self-efficacy can formally be defined as an individual's belief in his or her capacity to execute behaviors necessary to produce specific performance attainments. Confidence reflects in an employee's belief to get things done, to feel motivated, or to make decisions that will positively impact performance.

Optimism

Approaching everyday life with optimism provides a structure for shaping experiences through a lens of positivity. Activating feelings of optimism has been found to help individuals feel healthier, more committed to their work and less burned out.

Let me give you an example of positive behaviors in a selling situation. My wife and I recently were at Nordstrom's in the Twin Cities. She has a difficult time shopping for shoes because of her narrow feet. When we entered the shoe department of a large store, a salesperson greeted us immediately, thanked us for stopping in and asked my wife several questions about where we were from, what we were doing in town and what she was looking for. The salesperson showed empathy about my wife's shoe-shopping issues and related them to her own issues with having very wide feet.

As my wife looked at shoes, the salesperson went to the back and brought out several styles, then made several more trips to the back room until my wife finally settled on several and bought one pair.

In the end, the salesperson thanked us for stopping in and asked if we would like recommendations on where to eat and visit. Through this entire process, both my wife and I could tell that this salesperson was incredibly happy with her job, and we found it a pleasure to have her help us.

The salesperson displayed many positive behaviors. So, let me ask you again—would you rather buy from someone who is happy or someone that's miserable? Happiness and positive behaviors have a huge impact on sales effectiveness.

Too much, too little

One thing to keep in mind when you are looking at your top character strengths and positive behaviors is *balance*. It is very possible to use particular character strengths and positive behaviors too much or too little. Like Goldilocks, we want to find the balance that's just right.

Here is an example. My primary character strength is humor. If I use humor too much, then I am probably joking about everything. If I use it too little, then I can seem too serious about everything.

One of the best ways to analyze whether you are using your character strengths too much or too little is to ask three close friends what they think your top five character strengths are. Then match up their observations with your results from the VIA. If they are similar, then you are probably doing a pretty good job of keeping them in balance. But if they are completely different, then you need to examine how you are using them so as to bring them back in balance. When we use our character strengths and positive behaviors in balance, we are operating at peak performance, and we more easily act virtuously.

The Rule of Leading Oneself is all about how we act, both virtuously and positively, to impact our interactions with others. It's about doing the things you need to do for others so they will engage with you and allow you to build relationships with them. Now that we've talked about acting, let's move on to discuss using our strengths or talents at work.

Questions to Ask Yourself

1. What sales virtues are prevalent in my Character Strengths?

2. Am I using my character strengths in balance or am I using them too much or too little?

3. What positive behaviors can I use better to be a better salesperson?

Chapter 5
The Rule of Strengths (Talents)

Before I get into the Rule of Strengths, I'd like to begin by exposing various sales myths. Here is a typical ad that you can find on many help-wanted sites:

Looking for someone that has:

- A college degree.

- 3–5 years of experience.

- Personable sales professional.

- Unlimited income for those with the drive to succeed.

- Follow our step-by-step proven sales method.

So let's take a look at the sales myths that are implicit in the ad above.

Education: Bill Gates and Harry Truman never completed college. So much for education.

Experience: Josh Allen, Brock Purdy, Lamar Jackson and Patrick Mahomes, in their first two years, led their teams to the playoffs and pretty much crushed the theory that rookie quarterbacks needed experience to succeed. So much for experience.

A good salesperson can sell anything: Companies that change products or sales strategies can often experience unforeseen challenges. Simply having a good sales team doesn't mean they can sell anything at all.

Right sales approach: When you study exceptional salespeople, you find that they have developed their own approach that works best for them, yet we continue to try to make everyone do it the same way.

Training: The first sales training I went through was the Xerox training program in 1988. At the time, the Xerox program was considered the best in the country. The training taught us specific tactics, including trial closes, overcoming objectives, et cetera. But back then, the customer was a lot less informed. Information scientists have quantified all this. In 2011, Americans took in five times as much information every day as they did in 1986—the equivalent of 174 newspapers.

Today, during leisure time, each of us processes 34 GB or 100,000 words every day. The world's 21,274 television stations produce 85,000 hours of original programming per day, and we each watch an average of five hours of TV daily, the equivalent of 20 GB of images and audio. That's not counting YouTube, which uploads 6,000 hours of video every day, which is about 30,000 videos per hour.

If the training we do now doesn't match up with what's going on in the world, it's worthless. And with the amount of information out there, it is virtually impossible to match up training with information. I think training is way overblown!

Money: Gallup's research tells us that the number one motivation driver for people engaging at work is meaning and purpose in their work. In fact, money was sixth on the list.

Desire: Desire is only one part of the equation. When I was younger, I desired to be the next Jack Nicklaus. I worked hard at it and got myself to the point of giving it a shot, but my desire would only carry me so far. My lousy putting took care of my desire!

What are your sales strengths?

The StrengthsFinder® test, developed by the Gallup organization, first came into the public eye in 2001 thanks to the publication of *Now, Discover Your Strengths*. The self-help book was written by Marcus Buckingham and Donald Clifton, the chairman of Gallup. More than two million copies of the StrengthsFinder book were sold. Based on the notion that every person has certain strengths, StrengthsFinder identified and organized these strengths into thirty-four categories. Each of these falls into one of four domains called Executing, Influencing, Relationship Building, and Strategic Thinking. To compile all this information, the Gallup Organization initially interviewed more than 1.7 million professionals across a variety of fields. Gallup's research led to the development of categories, which they called "talent themes," but most people refer to them as strengths. The StrengthsFinder test identifies a person's top five strengths, and it is based on positive psychology, or what is "right" about people, not "wrong" with them.

I've had the opportunity to work with hundreds of salespeople and sales managers in over forty different industries using the StrengthsFinder. Based on the results I've seen, it is a tool that can transform sales organizations.

The sales strengths domains

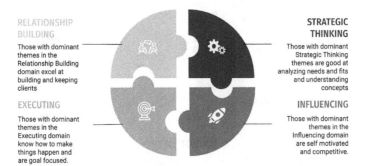

RELATIONSHIP BUILDING

Those with dominant themes in the Relationship Building domain excel at building and keeping clients

EXECUTING

Those with dominant themes in the Executing domain know how to make things happen and are goal focused.

STRATEGIC THINKING

Those with dominant Strategic Thinking themes are good at analyzing needs and fits and understanding concepts

INFLUENCING

Those with dominant themes in the Influencing domain are self motivated and competitive.

Relationship Building

This domain and the signature themes associated with it excel at building and keeping clients. The domain is about the talents needed to build relationships with clients. A person who is strong in this domain is excellent at these actions: listening, connecting with people and building positive relationships. This domain is also strong in networking and teamwork. People dominant in this theme are motivated by being with people and are energized by working with others. The Clifton StrengthsFinder themes that are associated with this domain are:

- Adaptability
- Connectedness
- Developer

- Empathy
- Harmony
- Includer
- Individualization
- Positivity
- Relator

Executing

The executing domain is about getting things done. The signature themes in this domain focus on process and how we get things done effectively and efficiently. Some of the energizing actions of this domain are focusing on our vision and purpose, managing time and consistently delivering results. People with signature themes in this domain are disciplined and orderly. They have great focus to accomplish goals and personally take responsibility for achieving those goals and not passing the buck. The Clifton Strengths themes in this domain are:

- Achiever
- Arranger
- Belief
- Consistency
- Deliberative
- Discipline

- Focus
- Responsibility
- Restorative

Strategic Thinking

The strategic thinking domain and its signature themes focus on analyzing needs and understanding concepts. People dominant in this theme are good at creating strategic plans, brainstorming and analyzing information. Salespeople in this domain typically excel in using CRM systems and utilizing the information from them to create game plans on how to approach customers and prospects. This domain is also about learning and putting knowledge to work. The Clifton Strengths themes in this domain are:

- Analytical
- Context
- Futuristic
- Ideation
- Input
- Intellection
- Learner
- Strategic

Influencing

The influencing domain—and the themes that attach to it—is the most natural one for many salespeople. This domain is all about connecting, persuading and getting people to follow through with a sale. In this domain, communicating and being able to convince people is easy and natural for people. When someone says they are a people person, they probably are strong in influencing. The Clifton Strengths associated with this domain are:

- Activator
- Command
- Communication
- Competition
- Maximizer
- Self-Assurance
- Significance
- Woo

The Clifton Strengths Report for Sales

In 2022 Gallup came out with a new report for salespeople using the StrengthsFinder tool. This report not only looks at the top five signature themes but also at what your next five themes are. Gallup claims that they "designed the report to make your days easier, bring clarity to your role and strengthen your sales effectiveness." It looks at each of the top ten themes and gives you ways that the theme can contribute to your success. It also offers ideas on how the theme might get in the way of your success if it's not being used in balance. The last part on each theme gives you specific recommendations and exercises to help you apply the theme to your work. After using the Clifton StrengthsFinder with hundreds of salespeople over the last twenty years, I can honestly say that I wish they had developed this report twenty years earlier. When combined with your character strengths and positive behaviors, it gives you all you need to exercise these in the best ways possible. So now let's bring them all together.

Putting the sales strengths to work

In the book *Strengths Based Selling* by Tony Rutigliano and Brian Brim, the authors identify the Strengths Equation. It is:

Talent (a natural way of thinking, feeling or behaving) x Investment (time spent practicing, developing your skills, and building your knowledge base) = Strengths (the ability to consistently provide near perfect performance).

The first step in putting your sales strengths to work is awareness. These strengths are constantly working in your subconscious. Now that you are aware of your signature themes, you can begin to consciously tap into them. You can start to recognize patterns in your work that fit your signature themes and also behaviors that make using your signature themes difficult. When I work with salespeople on these sales strengths, I want them to identify both the good and difficult things they do and then connect them to their themes.

In the case of difficult things, I want them to take a deep look at how their signature themes might help them navigate those difficulties. It may be that your signature themes show you are a relationship person but not very good at details. So, as you look at your top ten themes, are any of them ways to handle details better? The new Clifton StrengthsFinder for Sales Report mentioned earlier is a great tool for you to build awareness and understanding of how your sales strengths can help but also hinder you. In the next section, I'll give you some specific ideas of how to connect your character strengths, positive behaviors and sales strengths in your daily work.

Connecting character strengths, positive behaviors and talent themes, and understanding blind spots

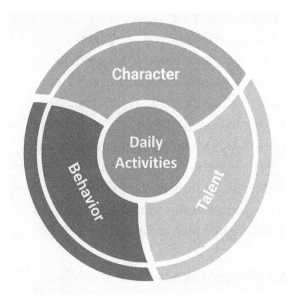

Connecting your character strengths, talents and behaviors is putting the Rule of Leading Oneself and the Rule of Strengths to work for you. How do you do that? The easiest way is to start documenting your daily activities—what specific things does your sales job require you to do, both customer-facing and internally? These could include presentations, prospecting, networking, attending sales meetings, doing paperwork, et cetera. Once you have completed the list, lay out your character strengths report, your Clifton Strengths for Sales Report and the graphic of positive behaviors in front of you. Go through all those daily activities and begin to map out all the strengths, talents and behaviors that coincide with each of those activities.

Once you have done that, look at those connections and honestly rate yourself on your balance using the strengths, talents and behaviors. Are you doing them too much in some activities or too little—or hopefully just right? The idea here is to grade yourself on how well you connect your work with your God-given character strengths, talents and positive behaviors. This gives you a baseline as you work through the rest of the Monk Principles© and will give you areas that you need to work on as you create your game plan at the end of the book.

Questions to ask yourself

1. Have I taken the Clifton StrengthsFinder?
   (if not, go to https://bit.ly/3nCjcbt.)

2. What surprised me about my sales strengths?

3. How can I use my sales strengths
   better in my work?

Chapter 6
The Rule of Excellence

The pursuit of excellence is a Benedictine hallmark. Benedict talks about the challenges of being a monk, but also about the drive, strength and the iron will it takes to bring their monasticism to perfection. He also talks about a different way than the world's way:

> Your way of acting should be different than the world's way; the love of Christ must come before all else. You are not to nurse a grudge. Rid your heart of all deceit. Never give a hollow greeting of peace or turn away when someone needs your love. Bind yourself to no oath lest it prove false, but speak the truth with the heart and tongue. (RB 4:20–27)

Benedict wants excellence in the monks and all they do. It's one of the reasons monasteries throughout the world are known for the quality in the things they make—for example, some of the best beers and liquors in the world.

Michael Jordan is arguably the greatest basketball player to ever play basketball, and though Jordan had immense talent, his drive for excellence was based on his understanding that talent still requires a person to work harder than anyone else. Jordan's intense work ethic is legendary, as reporters and former teammates often recount how the iconic athlete often competed as hard in practice as he did in actual games. One famous quote from Jordan sums up that ethos: "I don't do things half-heartedly. Because I know if I do, then I can expect half-hearted results."

The pursuit of excellence drives Benedictine monks just like it drove the greatest basketball player of all time. So, let's examine the Rule of Excellence. There are four aspects to this rule: focus/deep work, innovative thinking, creating your story and value creation. Let's take a closer look at these four aspects.

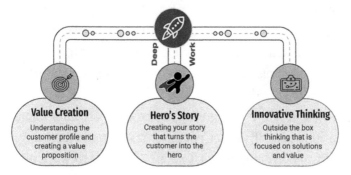

Deep work

There's a great book out there by Cal Newport called *Deep Work*. He outlines four different philosophies about what deep work might look like. The first one is the concept of the monastic system in which we eliminate or radically minimize shallow obligations and do one highly valued thing exceptionally well. This is a bit difficult to do because, normally, we're juggling many different balls and trying to make sure that we are able to execute on behalf of our different clients who need different solutions and strategies. So, this monastic concept is a little more difficult.

The next one is bimodal. Here we clearly define stretches for deep work. And then we leave the rest open to everything else and, and I use this a lot when I'm writing, where I will block out forty minutes or forty-five minutes and say okay, for the next forty or forty-five minutes, all I'm going to do is write, I'm not gonna look at email, I'm not gonna I'm gonna turn off the phone. All of those things. I'm just gonna focus on writing and what it is that I need to write, but I'll do it in short stints because what you find is that you know, we're easily distracted. And so if you can do this and say, Okay, I'm going to focus on this particular client or prospect or sale or whatever it is, for the next forty or forty-five minutes. That's all I'm going to work out. I'm not going to let any of the other distractions get to me. I'm going to turn off everything else, and then I can really do deep work regarding that.

The journalistic approach is where we fit in deep work wherever we can, and this one is very difficult to do. You really must have some practice. Doing it because it means that you sort of decided to do deep work sort of on the spot. You're thinking about a variety of different things, and all of a sudden, you say, okay, I've got to, I've got to focus on this one thing to get it done, and this one is much more difficult because it allows us to have those distractions you got to really work at practice this one and then the next one is down in the bottom there.

In the rhythmic approach, we transform deep work sessions into a regular habit at consistent times if you're really good at time management. This one works well if you can schedule it into your calendar and say, Okay, I'm going to, you know, from one o'clock to one forty-five,

I'm going to block out a time to focus on this particular thing. And I'm not going to let any of the distractions do it. The difference between rhythmic and bimodal is bimodal. You're just setting a timeframe of how long you're going to do it. Rhythmic is putting it into your calendar and doing it, and this works well with the reality of human nature because, especially in our sales environment, there are always going to be interruptions or things that come up that you need to deal with. If you've got it in your calendar, then you can self-manage and time-manage the things that go along with it. But one thing that's important to understand about this is that if we are not finding those times to do this deep work, it becomes very difficult to do the next couple of things that we're going to talk about which is creating value and innovative thinking. If you've got one hundred different distractions going on around you and you're trying to focus on a particular solution for a particular client, you're not going to be nearly as effective. If you're doing it just off the seat of your pants versus creating this deep work idea that allows you to focus on that particular solution or issue and take care of that client.

So deep work, being able to get into the rhythm of doing this, is really important. One of the things that I will say is that remote work can lend itself to this. I don't necessarily agree with having it all the time because we're human, and we want these social connections. We're social beings. And we want these social connections. So I think remote work has its downsides as well as its upsides. But I think one of the upsides is that it allows you to kind of shut everything else off and focus on this deep work without being interrupted by somebody walking in your office or somebody you know, popping their head in the door or whatever the case may be.

The deep work is a little bit easier to do when you're in this remote environment. So, it's something that I would really encourage you to think about. Think about, okay, how can I find those times when I'm most effective to do this, you know, and some of us also really need to understand that it may not be that eight to five timeframe. I'm much more effective writing in the evening than I am during the day.

Creating your hero's (customer) story

1   Who is your hero?

2   What is their problem?

3   Who will guide them and how?

4   Differentiation, what makes you stand out from the crowd

5   How do they take action?

6   What does their success look like?

The American writer Joseph Campbell first wrote about the "hero's journey" in 1949 in his book, *The Hero with a Thousand Faces*. He describes what is commonly known as the hero's journey. This process of creating a story is one that is used over and over again in books, movies and other literature. This same process can be used to create a sales story, your sales story. In his book, *Building a Story Brand*, Donald Miller says in the introduction,

> Your customer should be the hero in every story, not your brand. This is the secret that every phenomenally successful business understands.

Creating your sales story has a specific process that follows the "hero's journey." Here's what it looks like:

1. Who is your hero?
   a. Identifying your customer. What do they look like? What makes them tick? If you don't have a clear understanding of your customer, then you can't help them.
2. What is their problem?
   a. Next is to flesh out the problems, challenges, issues that your customer has. By understanding what their problems are, we can then think about solving them.

3. Finding a Guide
    a. All great movies have a hero and someone that helps them get where they are going. In *Lord of the Rings*, Gandalf is the guide for Frodo to help him return the ring and destroy it. The guide is you, helping your customer get from where they are to where they want to go.
4. Differentiating You as the Guide
    a. What makes you different? What are the characteristics of you, your brand, your product or service that is different from all the other ones out there? How does your process help them?
5. Call To Action
    a. How can someone use you? What specific steps can they take to work with you?
6. What does success look like for your hero?
    a. Once they have engaged with you, what does success look like? And most importantly, how has success transformed your hero? Luke Skywalker goes from being this young man on a quest to a Jedi knight saving the galaxy.

Creating your sales story is vital to your sales success. People only hear what you are saying if they can connect it to themselves, and the minute they can't, they're gone, and you've lost the opportunity. Using your story connects you to them.

Innovative Thinking

Innovative thinking is all about thinking outside of the way that we would normally think. It's about thinking differently in order to break through creative boundaries that don't allow us to solve problems creatively.

There is a great book by Adam Grant called *Think Again*. In this book, the author writes about how we typically think or speak in three different ways. We speak as a preacher as if we're trying to convert someone to our belief system. Or we speak and write as a prosecutor who is arguing his or her point to convince a jury of the guilt of a defendant. Or perhaps we speak or write as a politician who is trying to sweet talk an audience to win them over to his or her position.

Sometimes we behave like all three of these personas in the same conversation. I had a participant in one of my workshops confess to doing this. The first thing he told us was, "I just did this twenty minutes ago with my kid. First, I was the preacher trying to get her to believe it would be good for her to do something. Then I was the prosecutor arguing with her to get her to do something. And finally, I gave in and just gave her a reward for doing something."

So, we can perform as all three personas in one conversation. The author, Adam Grant, admonishes us to break out of that mentality and really start thinking like what he calls the philosopher or a scientist. If we begin to think like a philosopher or scientist, the first thing we do is doubt what we already know. And then we open up our minds to other ideas.

Without going down the perilous path of politics too much, if you think about what's going on in our world today, and especially as you connect it with social media, it becomes apparent that most of us tend to believe that our favorite social media sources tell us the absolute truth and anything else is incorrect. Well, the philosopher or the scientist would say, "You know, I'm not sure about that. I have some doubts about it."

Courageously confessing doubt leads us to the next step, which is curiosity. It's natural to be curious about what I don't know. And then, I began to explore other ideas and thoughts. I start listening to both sides of the equation. Curiosity allows us to open our minds to other ways of thinking.

The next step requires one of St. Benedict's key actions—exercising humility. Benedict talks about humility more in his Rule of Excellence than in any other chapter. Exercising humility is just admitting that we don't know everything. And if we don't know everything, it opens us up to new ideas and new ways of thinking that would have never been revealed to us before we doubted and developed curiosity.

The last step is discovery, which occurs as we explore other ideas and other people's perspectives. We then begin to discover new ways of thinking.

These steps are the foundation of innovative thinking. We have to understand that what we know today may be completely different from the knowledge awaiting our discovery. There may be a better way to look at a problem than how we're thinking about it, and so if we go through the process that Grant calls "rethinking," we begin to open up ways to do this, which opens up the whole concept of innovative thinking.

Based on this short summary, I have created a graphic called the possibility wheel. Remember those TV spots that begin with the tantalizing words, "What if…?" Those words begin the process of innovative thinking.

THE POSSIBILITY WHEEL: What if…?

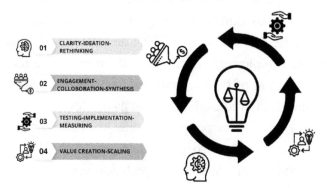

01 CLARITY-IDEATION-RETHINKING

02 ENGAGEMENT-COLLOBORATION-SYNTHESIS

03 TESTING-IMPLEMENTATION-MEASURING

04 VALUE CREATION-SCALING

The first step—even before using the possibility wheel—is clarifying what the issue, problem or challenge really is. Once we have clarity about that, we can begin to come up with solutions and rethink how we're approaching them from a sales perspective. We have to understand the issues faced by our prospects or clients. How can we help them solve their problems or meet their challenges?

Clarity starts with asking the right questions. What answers do we need for us to even get to the point where we can offer solutions? And then, we need to think like a philosopher or scientist in order to make sure that we understand the true nature of their issues.

Once we get clarity, then step 1 on the possibility wheel is to begin to ideate and brainstorm, to rethink how we might solve this issue, problem or challenge.

This creative process leads us to step 2, which is engagement. Here we take our ideas and possible solutions to others. We engage with our team to fine-tune and update the ideas and determine how we can implement them. We collaborate on further clarification of the problem and look for alternative solutions offered from other points of view.

From a sales perspective, this team engagement is critical because, so often, salespeople are sort of stranded on an island and expected to come up with solutions in isolation. But collaboration often stimulates better ideas, which moves us to the next step.

Step 3 is implementation of our ideas and measuring their results. Eric Ries wrote a book called *Lean Startup* in which he explains that startups usually begin with a "minimally viable product" or MVP. Based on that MVP, the entrepreneur and his or her team comes up with the simplest solution that can be implemented quickly with the fewest resources and can be measured in a meaningful way.

The next step for a startup is to execute this MVP, which can be a product or an idea, a program, a market or any number of things. The MVP is just the minimal concept. This is the time where the team tests if they have a solution? Will it work? If it won't work well, then we toss it on the junk heap and move on to the next possible solution.

If it does work, however, and it looks to be a viable solution, then we can move to the next step of scaling it and creating value. At this point, the team begins to roll it out across the organization. And so this value creation and scaling helps determine if the MVP really solves the big picture issue.

The process identified in the possibility wheel allows us to think outside the box to come up with different solutions that perhaps we hadn't thought about. This is innovative thinking made tangible from the perspective of the Rule of Excellence.

Creating customer value

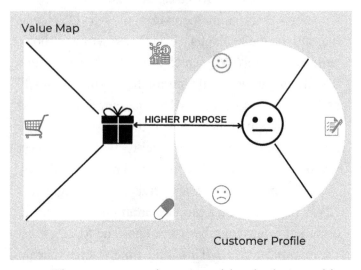

The customer value proposition is the next big concept we need to master. In the customer-value proposition, you get more detailed on how your product or service will interact with the customer. You've created your story earlier—now we want to switch to thinking about value for the customer. Here we are going to focus solely on your product or service and how it adds value to the customer. The diagram above is an adaptation from the book *Value Proposition Design*, a Strategyzer series book. The idea is to connect a customer profile with our products and solutions. The circle on the right shows that you have customer jobs, which is basically just laying out what your typical customer or your preferred customer looks like. Who do you really want to have as a customer? It's important to list the customer's important characteristics. Is it a different type of business? Is it a person who has particular things that you connect better with? What are their roles in their organizations?

Maybe the customer is the end user, maybe a buyer, perhaps a business owner. Understanding their roles allows you to identify their pains. Below, to the left, you can see the pains. What pain points plague this customer? What are the things your customers deal with that really are a pain in their necks and cause them to say, "This is what I'm dealing with on a daily basis and I'm looking for solutions."

And then, up on top are the gains. What benefits can the customer receive if they do business with you? What are their potential gains?

This customer profile helps you begin to create value in the solutions you offer to that customer. If we look at the box on the left side, you've got your products and services. These are all of the various solutions you could provide to that particular customer. And then, as you look at each one, you can decide if it's either going to be a pain reliever or a gain creator. Sometimes they're both, but most of the time they're going to be one or the other.

One of my clients provides financing for small businesses. In looking at a particular financing situation, perhaps a loan allows the customer to manage cash flow better. That would be a pain reliever. Maybe the loan will give them the capital to construct a new building that may actually be a gain creator. This is why you need to connect your customer's situation with your products in a meaningful way.

The last step is to factor in a connection to higher purpose—something that's bigger than both your organization and the customer. You can see the line that connects the two areas. When we factor in a connection of higher purpose we really begin to create value.

The Rule of Excellence gets us to begin deep work in thinking about our story, our customers, our value proposition and how we solve problems with each individual customer. It helps us move people from one idea to the next, providing a basis for solving their problems and being successful salespeople.

100

Questions to ask yourself

1. What was the last innovative idea you had and how did it get implemented?

2. What is your hero's story?

3. Have you connected your ideal customer to your value proposition?

Chapter 7
The Rule of Order (Statio)

The Rule of Order is where we clearly define the sales process. Benedict, in his "Rule," believes that everything has order and that order leads to stability. Everything in the monastery is a process—when the monks wake up, when they eat, when they pray and when they work. Everything has a time and place. Unfortunately, many sales organizations and people miss this idea of process or order, or they mandate an order for unimportant activities that do not contribute to success.

Many times I've asked sales managers to describe their sales process and they look at me like a deer caught in the headlights and mumble something like, "We sell the features and benefits of our product or service, that's our process."

What are the key components of an effective sales process?

1. Focused on the customer: The process must be completely focused on the customer and what they need and want.

2. Repeatable: The process must be repeatable and teachable so that salespeople understand the process and can be trained on the process.

3. Flexible: The process can be flexible enough so that each salesperson can play to their strengths and talents and do what they do best.

4. Measurable: The process is measurable, and goals are able to be set in order to determine success and failure.

The sales process must incorporate what happens before the sale, during the sale and after the sale. Salespeople need to understand that selling isn't just about making the sale, it's the journey through the selling process and about creating relationships with customers/clients. But before we start the sales process, let's talk about preparation.

What is statio?

The monastic traditions have what they call "statio." In her book *Wisdom Distilled from the Daily: Living the Rule of St. Benedict Today,* author Joan Chitisster describes "statio," which she so aptly calls the "virtue of presence."

In addition to silence, community customs, and the common table, the monastic practices of statio and lectio are also tools of the spiritual craft. Statio is a monastic custom that was born centuries ago but clearly belongs in this one. Statio is the practice of stopping one thing before we begin another. It is the time between times. It is a cure for the revolving door mentality that is common in a culture that runs on wheels. In monastic spirituality it is common for the community to gather outside of chapel in silence before beginning prayer or at least to gather for a few minutes together in the chapel itself before intoning the opening hymn of the Office.

The idea of stopping one thing before we begin another is one of the most important principles of sales excellence. This "taking pause" is a principle that most salespeople never consider before running headlong into a sales meeting or presentation. They fly into an appointment fresh off another phone call from another client or prospect, or they move from a frustrating meeting with their sales manager right into a sales presentation, never considering that the prospect will clearly sense their foul mood. The practice of statio is meant to center us and make us conscious of what we're about to do—to make us present to the task at hand. Statio is the desire to do consciously what I might otherwise do mechanically or unconsciously. But the idea of taking pause to make sure we're ready is part of the sales process. "Sales Statio" covers four aspects as part of the preparation before the sales meeting.

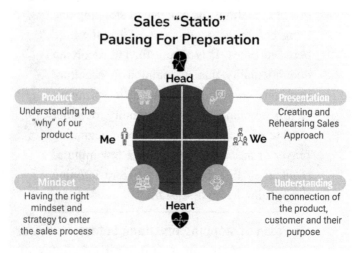

Sales "Statio"
Pausing For Preparation

The first aspect is understanding the "why" of your product or service. Why should the prospect listen to you describe your product or service? This understanding of your product is crucial because you don't want to find out something about your product in the middle of the presentation. Having a clear understanding of what you're selling and why it's good for the prospect seems like common sense, but I've seen many salespeople go into meetings unprepared to cover the details about what they are selling.

Presentation

The second aspect is mapping out what your presentation will encompass and how it will flow. I've been with salespeople who have their presentations all over the place and jump from concept to concept until they have the prospect so confused there is no chance they will buy. I've been with other salespeople that just wing it. They don't even have an outline of what they want to cover, relying on luck and intuition that they might say the right thing to get the client to buy.

Understanding

The third aspect of "sales statio" is understanding. This is where you make the connection between the product or service you have and what the prospect needs, making sure that you are connecting the dots in your presentation. This requires going back through your notes about the customer to make sure you completely understand where the prospect is today versus where you want them to be after the sale. Your goal is to connect their needs and wants to what you have.

This is where the features and benefits approach to selling misses the point. If all you are trying to do is convince someone to buy based on product features and benefits you've missed the opportunity to connect needs, wants, solutions and peace of mind to the sales approach.

Mindset

The fourth aspect of "sales statio" is your own mindset. Here you connect the dots on how you will approach this sales meeting or presentation, getting your mind in the right frame to be able to listen effectively and communicate accurately. Your mindset encompasses how you feel, what your expectations are for the meeting, how you will handle objections and what the result of the sale can do for your prospect. If you create this mindset for yourself, then there is no way to fail, because even if the sale doesn't occur you have the opportunity to learn from the meeting and create a better approach next time. I often tell financial services salespeople that after a sales call that didn't go well, don't think of it as a failure but as an opportunity to practice—and that practice will lead to future success.

Other aspects of "sales statio" involve connecting your head and your heart and also looking at the sales meeting in terms of *me* and *we*. What do I mean by connecting head and heart? Some of the things we cover in a sales meeting are driven by the head—our knowledge of our product or service, our presentation, and how it's put together. Other parts of our sales meeting are driven by our hearts, our understanding of where the prospect is and our mindset in handling our emotions and feelings.

The sales meeting also connects *me* and *we*. There are parts that the salesperson brings to the meeting such as a presentation of product information and personal mindset. But the sales conversion is between your prospect and you—your understanding of their needs and the customer's understanding of how your product and service will meet their needs.

The idea to take a pause for preparation before a sale can benefit any salesperson, even when the prospect approaches you as in a retail selling situation. Quickly taking a pause before pouncing on them—evaluating what you see, your own mindset, what they might be looking for and how you might connect with them—will give you a genuineness that the prospect will notice and connect with. "Sales statio" is one of the most important aspects of creating sales excellence.

The Monk Principles© sales process

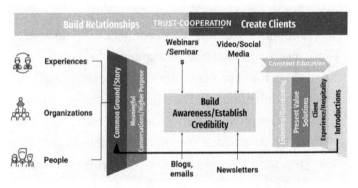

Order and stability in a monastic community is of the highest importance. Benedict talks about the Gyrovague monks who go from monastery to monastery looking for greener grass. The Cenobite monks, however, stay with one monastery and follow the order and Abbot to become their best selves.

How many salespeople do you know who are gyrovagues always looking for something better. Unfortunately, one of the things that drives salespeople to continually search for a better opportunity is that the company they work for is out of touch or out of date with the times.

With those distinctions in mind, let's talk about the many components of the Monk Principles© sales process. Many sales organizations and salespeople are already implementing some of these components, but the *order* of the components is what I want to emphasize.

Build Relationships

At the top, we have Build Relationships, which comes before Create Clients. This suggests the best order for those two steps. Many salespeople today do these things in the opposite order, starting with a product instead of building relationships, which means they think the product will help build a relationship. I think that's backwards! So how do we start building relationships?

We put into place a specific process focused on the value we can provide to our prospects and clients. The starting point of that process is common ground.

Common Ground

We start with what I call common ground. This is where we begin to establish a relationship. Common ground is a connection between the experiences you have, the organizations you belong to and the people you associate with. Before you ever have a conversation with a prospect, you must identify common ground.

The key to establishing common ground is the primary discussion. It is too early for your product or service to come into play. Common ground should fit right in with your purpose! In many cases, common ground has to do with hospitality or, as the Benedictines would say, breaking bread. It is so much easier to find common ground while breaking bread, whether that's breakfast, lunch, dinner, or an evening drink. That's when people are much more open to conversations.

My form of common ground was always the golf course, which provided an informal opportunity to connect with a prospect, but you also get to see them in a different environment over an extended period of time.

Meaningful conversations

After establishing common ground, we can begin to have meaningful conversations with people about their lives and their challenges. By having these meaningful conversations, we can develop our understanding about how we can help them. We also can connect our higher purpose with them to see if that extends our common ground. Connecting this higher purpose also shows people that what you are doing is not for a selfish purpose but for reasons that are bigger than yourself.

Trust and Cooperation

The first two steps in this process begin to create something that is vital in every selling interaction and that creates trust. People won't buy from you if they don't trust you. So many salespeople skip right over this and move onto the product and the solution it solves but you can have the greatest product in the world and if people don't trust you then they won't buy it, no matter how good it is. Once people begin to trust you then they also begin to cooperate with you and they start allowing you to educate them and to find out what their needs are and how you can help them. Without this trust and cooperation your sales efforts are dead in the water. The best way to create this trust and cooperation is through the positive behavior we talked about earlier, empathy. When people feel that you are empathetic to your situation then they will begin to trust you.

Creating awareness

Once we've established common ground and had some meaningful conversations, then we can begin the process of creating awareness. In creating awareness, we do two things. We help the prospect start to identify how we could help them and also establish our credibility to do that. While this can be done through numerous marketing tactics, at no time do we talk about specific products. These communications are entirely conceptual and educational. The tools we use— webinars, emails, videos, social media posts, blogs and podcasts— give us an opportunity to build credibility. One point of caution here though—if you are relying on your organization to do these things you are missing the chance to enhance your personal credibility. Most prospects won't connect your company with you, so make sure you are part of these marketing tactics.

Active listening/questioning

The next step is to find opportunities to help them identify blind spots and pain points. This used to be called fact finding, but it should be part of an active conversation, not running down a checklist to get their information. The financial services industry is notorious for providing salespeople with fact finders and checklists to get information, but these impersonal lists take the focus off having an active conversation and risks turning the process into a robotic capturing of data.

Through an interpersonal conversation we ask questions and actively listen. Prospect should be speaking 80 percent of the time and the salesperson 20 percent, which is the opposite of what many salespeople do. As they present all the features and benefits, they forget to uncover whether those features provide the benefits the prospect needs.

Identifying gaps, blind spots and needs

While actively listening, we can ask pointed questions that help us discover where the prospect's gaps and blind spots are, which in turn helps us formulate how we can help them.

Presenting solutions/ideas

Once we have helped the prospect understand their gaps, blind spots and needs, we are finally in a position to present a solution, idea or concept focused on value and peace of mind for the prospect. In presenting our solution, we first practice "sales statio" so we are completely prepared for the presentation.

When I create a new seminar, I always write out the speaker notes completely and then repeatedly go over those notes so I automatically know what the next slide will be. This way I can react to audience questions instead of figuring out where I am. "Sales statio" helps me prepare for any possible query or interruption that can occur.

Customer experience/hospitality

If the proposed solution is accepted, the prospect now becomes a customer. Most salespeople stop here thinking their job is done. But if you really want to build relationships, you now take the customer's hand and walk them through the final delivery of their product or service, educating them along the way so they know exactly what to expect as the process unfolds.

My wife is great at doing this. As a real estate agent, once she has a signed contract she knows that the work has only begun, so she is constantly updating the client on where they are in the buying or selling process, and what to expect next. That's probably why 95 percent of her business comes from referrals.

This step is creating a positive customer experience. Every aspect of your process must be as painless for the customer as possible, and it's critical to keep the customer educated on every step to the outcome. I'll present more about creating this customer experience in the next rule.

Introductions

Once you have created that customer experience and developed a strong client relationship you can ask for introductions to others. When you get an introduction, you go back to the beginning—common ground—with that new prospect. You also want to stay in front of your established customers to continue creating value, providing education and building the relationship so that the customer wants to do business with you again and introduce you to others.

Many sales organizations suggest doing some of these steps, but their training is mostly on the tactics of the process, such as fact finding, presenting features and benefits, and closing sales. If organizations develop salespeople on the whole process—not just parts of it—salespeople create real value for their customers, build long-term relationships and have a much better chance at success.

Here are the challenges to this process that you should be aware of:

- This process is slower, but it builds deeper connections.

- This process must link marketing concepts and education, not products

- This process must be built on the salesperson's individual strengths, talents and behaviors and the organization's higher purpose, which takes more training and development work.

Questions to ask yourself

1. Do you have a clearly defined process for selling?

2. What common ground do you have with others?

3. How can you practice sales "statio?"

Chapter 8
The Rule of Community

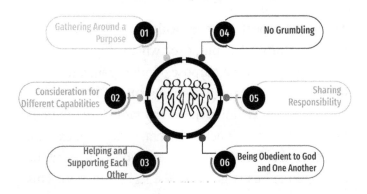

01 Gathering Around a Purpose	04 No Grumbling
02 Consideration for Different Capabilities	05 Sharing Responsibility
03 Helping and Supporting Each Other	06 Being Obedient to God and One Another

The next monk principle is the Rule of Community. Community is one of the most important hallmarks of the Benedictines. The Rule of Benedict is all about how we live and work in community. The Rule provides a blueprint for monasteries and abbeys to use in living and working together. Jane Tomaine's book, *St. Benedict's Toolbox,* identifies some of the aspects of a Benedictine community that are in the diagram above. I believe that six of these aspects also relate to sales.

Seen from a sales perspective, as salespeople we are not on an island. We have a group of individuals in our organization who are our team. But in order for that team to support us at its peak capability, we need to understand some basic principles regarding this idea of community as it relates to sales teams.

Gathering around a purpose

The first aspect of the Rule of Community is gathering around a purpose, which requires a full understanding of the purpose of our organization. We have talked about purpose in the Rule of Purpose and Vision, which is aimed at the individual, but there is also a community function to that. When a sales team is gathered around a purpose, everyone is aboard the bus, and the bus is going in the right direction. This team approach to purpose connects everyone and solidifies the community. When everyone is focused on the same purpose, there is no internal competition, and everyone is working together toward the common goal.

Differing capabilities

The second aspect is the recognition that each person on the team has different capabilities. Everybody has different strengths and varying talents. Some people may not be equipped to help us with a particular client or solution. But they can offer useful suggestions or encouragement or share relevant experience. Regarding this, Benedict writes about assigning duties to those that are capable, with the strongest monks getting the most difficult jobs and those lesser monks getting jobs that fit their abilities. This makes each of the monks feel good about their contributions. Sales teams have people with many different capabilities, but for the team to succeed, each member of the community has to do their share toward the team effort.

Supporting and helping each other

The third aspect is helping and supporting each other, from a standpoint of getting the most in the best out of the organization. Sometimes that means that we have to set aside our own activities and sales pursuits to help somebody else. Another salesperson may need your experience or wisdom or ideas. This may not directly help you in your sales endeavors, but it encourages other members of the team to help you when you need it.

No grumbling

The fourth aspect Benedict writes about is no grumbling. I have seen grumbling completely tear apart sales organizations. It can be a cancer. Understanding that grumbling contributes nothing is essential for the smooth operation of the team. In the Rule, Benedict is very practical. He even addresses the proper amount of drink, and he talks about grumbling:

> However where local circumstances dictate an amount less stipulated… or even none at all, those who live there should bless God and not grumble. Above all else we admonish them to refrain from grumbling. (RB 40: 8–9)

We have to set that aside. If we continue to hear the same grumbling repeatedly, that becomes a little different story because it may mean there is an issue to deal with. Then, the issue must be addressed by an assigned individual. For the most part, though, negativity, when expressed as grumbling, wrecks morale and slows down the entire team.

Sharing responsibility

The fifth aspect is sharing responsibility. I wrote earlier about not passing the buck—making sure that we're taking responsibility for our own actions and taking responsibility for the things that need to be done. But in a community, many responsibilities must be shared and shared willingly. So, it's a give and take. Often, sharing responsibility is how we make sure that we're getting done what needs to get done, but also how we give others the opportunity to contribute what they can.

Obedient to each other

The last aspect is being obedient to one another. This is about respecting each other, respecting the fact that everyone has their gifts and talents, and that if we are respectful or obedient to one another, we all thrive. The ship rises in this rising tide. Being obedient to each other gives us the opportunity to be truly engaged as a sales team and understand that we're all here for the good of the organization, of ourselves, and, most importantly, of our customers.

Very few salespeople are successful without some sort of community to help them. Building a healthy community to support your sales efforts is essential to sales flourishing.

Questions to ask yourself

1. Do you treat your sales team like community?

2. What could you do to create better community in your sales team?

3. Do you grumble? And if so, is there a better way to handle it?

Chapter 9
The Rule of Hospitality

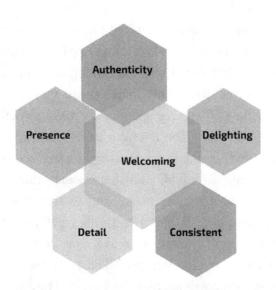

Let me tell you about the $2.00 hotdog.

This story originated in the book *Unreasonable Hospitality* by Will Guidara. Will is the co-owner of

11 Madison, which has been the top restaurant in New York City for nine years. In the book, he tells about a table of women who were chatting over dinner in his restaurant. Will could overhear their conversation and learned they were in New York City for a girls' weekend. Their intent was to eat at some of the best restaurants in New York City, and 11 Madison was their last stop. Over time, the women discussed some of the fine meals they'd had and the high quality of service they'd enjoyed, but then one of the women said, "But we didn't get a New York hotdog! How could we miss that?"

On a lark, Will ran into the kitchen, gave one of his chefs some cash and asked him to run down the street to the nearest food cart and bring back a genuine New York hot dog. Once the hotdog was procured, Will had to convince his James Beard-winning chef to take the $2.00 entree and quickly make something special out of it. The chef cut the wiener into five pieces and created an artistic masterpiece with ketchup, mustard, pickle relish and sauerkraut.

Will brought the platter out to the table and told the women, "I heard you didn't get your New York hotdog. I wanted to make sure you got that experience, so here you go." The response that he got from these women blew him away. They had just finished a five-star, award-winning dinner, but they were enthralled with the $2.00 hotdog.

> "It struck me that you can have the greatest food and best experience in the world, but if you're not doing something that goes beyond that, you're not creating unreasonable hospitality." That became the subject of his book—unreasonable hospitality.

I often talk about the Starbucks customer experience. When Starbucks first started, the idea was simply to sell coffee. The concept was to create a place where someone could come and have a conversation with another person over a cup of great coffee in a warm and comfortable environment. Howard Schultz, the founder of Starbucks, had gotten this epiphany while he was visiting Europe and experiencing all the little sidewalk cafes where people would sit for two hours and have a conversation over coffee. Starbucks became the first coffee chain to create this kind of experience. Until the coming of covid, Starbucks was the number one business meeting place in the world. More people had meetings in a Starbucks than anywhere else. By offering that experience, Starbucks became who they are today.

Hospitality has been around for thousands of years. Benedict wrote that hospitality was such a hallmark for the Benedictines that even when a guest would show up at the abbey or at the monastery, everything would be dropped. All focus would be on the guest, who would feel like they were the only person there. In the Rule, Benedict says:

Once a guest is announced, the superior and the brothers are to meet him with all the courtesy of love. (RB 53:3)

As we look at hospitality in the sales environment, hospitality is more than customer service. When properly understood and implemented, it can help us clearly differentiate who we are against our competitors. It starts with this idea of welcoming.

Welcoming

Are we welcoming to those who approach us or those who we approach? Do we truly want to develop a relationship with them? Welcoming occurs when we open ourselves up to a prospect and make them feel like they're the only one in the room. That's the first step in delivering hospitality.

Welcoming makes the customer or prospect want to have a conversation with you. It shows them you care about them being there with you at that moment. Welcoming starts with the simplest thing—a smile. I have seen many salespeople walk into meetings, and by their expressions, you would think they were entering the room for a root canal.

When you smile, not only do you feel good about yourself, but people smile back, which makes them feel better too. When someone asks my wife how she is, her response is always, "I'm happy. How are you?" Now that's what I call welcoming.

Authenticity

The next essential ingredient of hospitality is authenticity. How many times have you received a Christmas gift and thought, "They sure put a lot of thought into this." All of us have received such thoughtful gifts and understood the gift-giver's authenticity they represent. Authenticity in words and actions means they were spoken or done for the sole purpose of that individual. When we take the time to be conscious about hospitality, we don't just take the quick and easy way out. We find a way to show authenticity.

Presence

The next principle of hospitality is presence, which gets back to the concept of positive behavior. We have learned about active listening and empathy. Being present, however, goes beyond that. It involves not being distracted—not thinking about seven other things while we're trying to have a conversation with a prospect or client. Presence is about coming to the individual and making sure you know everything is now about them and that you are zeroed in on their needs and interests.

Detail

Another aspect of hospitality is detail. It is imperative to "sweat the details," like the $2.00 hotdog that was turned into a work of art. We must make sure that everything we do is down to the finest detail, whether it is a presentation, delivering a particular product or just thanking someone for doing business with you. Sweat the details and make sure that every one of them is up to snuff. The details move beyond simply creating customer service or customer experience.

Consistency

Another aspect is consistency. You can't just do it once. You have to continually do it over and over and over again, and deliver it from a consistent standpoint.

Surprise and delight

The last aspect is to find ways to surprise and delight, just like Will did when he brought out that $2.00 hotdog. Surprising and delighting a prospect or customer is like closing a sale.

Enlightened Hospitality

In restaurateur Danny Meyer's book *Setting the Table*, the author talks about enlightened hospitality, which he explains is about discovering the right order of who is the most important target of your hospitality. Meyer describes in the following order five potential stakeholders in enlightened hospitality:

- Employees
- Guests
- Community members
- Suppliers
- Investors

Meyer's restaurants are some of the most successful in the country, including Shake Shack and Union Square Cafe in New York City. He suggests that when the order happens, the profits at the end make the investors happy. All decisions are made based on that order.

What might that look like for a salesperson? How could we create a ranked order of stakeholders that might lend itself to the type of success Meyer has created?

I would propose that to create enlightened hospitality in sales, the order would be:

- Family
- Prospect/Customer

- Sales Support Team
- Product/Service Team
- Salesperson

The first stakeholder in my ranking of importance is the salesperson's family. If the work of the salesperson is detrimental to his or her family life, do you think that salesperson is operating at peak performance and wisely using personal strengths and talents? Here, positive behaviors include making time for family and making sure family members are taken care of.

The second stakeholder on my ordered list seems obvious—the customer or prospect, without whom there are no sales.

The third stakeholder is the sales support team, which could include inside sales support, marketing, sales assistants, et cetera. If the salesperson takes care of these individuals and understands the Rule of Community, these people all become an asset.

The fourth stakeholder is the team that actually creates and delivers the product or service, which may be in-house or a vendor. Maintaining a good relationship with these individuals is vital to products and services being delivered as promised.

The last stakeholder is the individual salesperson. I know this flies in the face of many sales training programs and organizations. But I can tell you from experience that if a salesperson is doing all they can do to build up the first four stakeholders, that salesperson will be wildly successful.

Going back to the Rule of Leading Oneself— when we act with virtue and do the right things, good things happen. When we use our character strengths, talents and positive behaviors to provide enlightened hospitality, we set ourselves up for sales flourishing.

Questions to ask yourself

1. How do you deliver hospitality to your customers and prospects?

2. Do you have specific things you do that surprise and delight?

3. Are you consistent with being a welcoming and authentic presence?

Chapter 10
Mapping Your Success

What can you do to initiate this type of sales process and development? The first thing is to bring everything together—to create your own rule for selling. How are you going to put together these seven monk principles that you've learned? To create your own rule for selling, go back and look at the answers to the questions at the end of each chapter. Pick out one idea from each of the seven monk principles that deeply resonated with you. Start with these small steps to craft a game plan that will lead eventually to putting all the principles to work. When you pick out those key points that you feel strongest about, you will be creating your own framework for a comprehensive sales system.

The sales planning funnel

Let's start connecting the monk principles to your work. How are you going to do that? As we create this game plan, constantly think about how we're connecting these monk principles to what you're doing from a sales perspective.

The first step is what I call the sales planning funnel. In 2008, I wrote a book called *Ultimate Breakthrough Planning: The Business Funnel Approach*. I laid out a funnel process for creating a business. I have now tweaked that concept to fit a sales perspective.

Higher purpose vision

As you can see in this diagram, the first step is what we call higher purpose goals, or your vision. What is it you want to achieve? What is your vision for the next six months?

Why six months? I have found that if you create a plan and work it for six months, you can easily get it done and measure it. Things can change quickly. Consider how quickly covid was upon us—everybody's sales plans went out the window when that happened. So, create a six-month plan, then assess it and then add new or additional strategies for the next six months. This makes each plan very doable.

Strategies

Once we have a clear vision of what you want, we can begin to break things down into the things that will help you achieve that vision, including the monk principles we've talked about.

The second step is identifying strategies. A strategy may be concepts, new markets, new industries, customer targets, products or services. Maybe it's one of the monk principles. Perhaps it's doing hospitality better. You don't want more than about four strategies, or you are never going to get them done. I've worked through this process with literally hundreds of businesses and several thousand salespeople, and if you have more than four strategies, you're going to be overwhelmed.

Tactics, tasks, timelines

Once you've figured out your strategies, we break them down into the planning wheel tactics. I will talk more about that shortly. Once we have identified our tactics, we break those down into tasks and timelines. These items are for our weekly to-do list. What do I need to get accomplished this week to make sure these planning wheel tactics and strategies are happening?

Key milestones

The last piece is to identify key milestones. Rather than focusing on the goal, focus on the activities that are necessary to reach those higher purposes and vision. These key milestones are not results-based, so they cannot be sales, commissions or profits. They are the activities you need to accomplish to get results using the monk principles. These key milestones are the planning wheel tactics that we will measure.

The Planning Wheel

PLANNING WHEEL: TACTICS

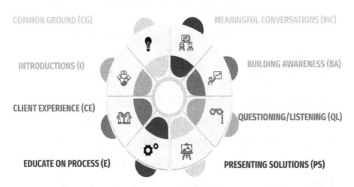

In this diagram, I've placed the eight different areas we talked about in the sales process. The first one is common ground. What can I do to connect my common ground to potential prospects and clients? Can I use an organization that I belong to? Can I leverage experiences that I'm participating in? Maybe there are relationships with vendors that I already know. The biggest thing to understand between common ground and prospecting is that common ground gives you that warm lead. Common ground gives you something that already connects with your prospect or customer. It is NOT trying to get someone to have a conversation with you— you've already got common ground to do that.

As we go around the wheel to the right, we hit meaningful conversations.

What are they?

How many of those do we need?

The next step is building awareness. This is where we go to marketing and say, "These are some of the tactics we need to begin creating awareness and building credibility. This step also begins to educate the prospect on what they don't know so they start the initial step of finding their own blind spots. There are going to be a lot of things here that you can do and collaborate on with the marketing department. Remember, this is not just the marketing department's responsibility. The salesperson also needs to take the initiative and do their own personal branding to build awareness.

The next step is questioning and listening. Who are the individuals we're talking to? What are the specific questions we need to have answered before we can suggest a solution?

Next is presenting solutions. How many different presentations are we going to do? How can we better prepare for presentations? How do I incorporate "sales statio?"

The next piece is educating on the process. What does this mean in my business and in the customer's business? Am I doing a good job in educating on the process so that the customer understands what the next step is? How long is it going to take? Make sure we've got expectations set so that the prospect or customer doesn't think something's going to happen in two weeks when it will really take six.

The next step is enhancing the client experience and improving the hospitality aspect of it. What can we do to build and create this?

The last step is getting introductions to others with common ground.

Planning Worksheets

The planning worksheets I describe here can be downloaded at https://tinyurl.com/2pshcfxr.

The first planning sheet is the sales planning funnel. This sheet has all the different colored blocks on it. This is really your overall strategic action plan. Here you're going to walk through the funnel for creating your higher purpose goals/vision, strategies, planning, wheel tactics, tasks and timelines, and key milestones.

Your Game Plan
Higher Purpose Goals
Strategies
Planning Wheel Tactics
Tasks/Timelines
Key Milestones

Next is the weekly activity sheet. This tool lays out a weekly process using the planning wheel tactics.

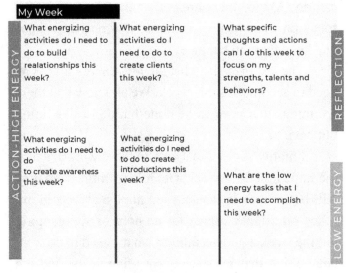

When you view this sheet, you can see that on the left-hand side are action and high-energy things that you can do. What energizing activities do I need to do to build relationships this week? What energizing activities do I need to do to create awareness this week? What energizing activities do I need to do to create clients this week? And what energizing activities do I need to do to create introductions this week?

On the right-hand side, list your specific thoughts and actions that you can do this week to focus on your strengths, talents and behaviors. What are your character strengths? What are your positive behaviors? What are your talents, strengths, Clifton Strengths and themes? What are the things that you can do? Maybe there are one or two things you can focus on this week to continue to strengthen those and keep them in balance.

The last piece is to list the low-energy tasks you need to accomplish this week. We all know that there are things that need to be done but don't like doing but have to.

I highly suggest that you do these worksheets at the same time each week. Get into a routine, and they will become easier to do. I am almost always in my office on Sunday nights for an hour or so, mapping out the week and determining what I need to do. I've been doing that for over twenty-five years, and it's become a habit. When I'm traveling and don't do it, I feel guilty.

Here are some examples of high-energy tasks. While attending a networking event, which you enjoy, you begin cultivating common ground and building relationships. Or maybe you like meeting one-on-one with people over coffee, and that gives you energy. If you think about those simple tasks from the perspective of what you really love about your job, you have uncovered high-energy tasks. What do I really love to do? Is it connecting with clients and prospects? They are the things you thrive on and can't wait to get out of bed in the morning to get started on.

You don't like doing the low-energy stuff but

have no choice about doing it. When I was working with financial advisors, I was not a detail guy, so for me making sure the paperwork and reports were completed were low-energy tasks. During covid, when the world shut down, it had a significant negative impact on me. I wanted to be out meeting people and having conversations, but then, all of a sudden, we were isolated. I was relegated to doing mostly those low-energy tasks I hated. Needless to say, when things started opening up again, I was thrilled to be able to start doing those high-energy tasks I enjoyed.

Creating your game plan and using the activity sheets are ways to keep you on track and to make sure the whole sales system is front and center in your work. There will always be a few things that may throw you off track, but the sooner you get back to using these tools, the more success you will have. Over the years, I've measured how salespeople have utilized these tools, and I can honestly say that those who stick with it and work their plans consequently grow their sales by 27 percent each year. That's sales flourishing!

Questions to ask yourself

1. Define your vision and what
   you want to achieve.

2. Create your rule for selling. Does it
   include all the monk principles?

3. Would creating a game plan and
   using the weekly worksheet put you
   on a better track for success?

Chapter 11
The Rules for Managers, Mentors and Coaches

Every great athlete attributes their greatness to a coach somewhere along the line. Most sales organizations use the sales manager approach, and usually, that manager was formerly an excellent salesperson. Unfortunately, as I've discovered over years of working with salespeople and their managers, great salespeople rarely make great sales managers. Also, for some reason, sales organizations often fail to distinguish between mentors, coaches and sales managers, so they miss out on the value of these three different kinds of influence. Benedict addresses management in the Rule when he talks about the qualities of the abbot:

> Furthermore, anyone who receives the name of abbott is to lead disciples by a twofold teaching: he must point out to them all that is good and holy more by example than by words, proposing the commandments of the Lord... but demonstrating God's instructions to the stubborn and the dull by a living example. (RB 2:11–12)

Benedict's idea of managing is about teaching and leading by example and I know many sales managers that could use that advice.

Mentoring

Putting seasoned sales professionals with newer sales professionals is a great way to give the new people support and let the experienced pros share their knowledge. But for this situation to work, some guidelines need to be put into place.

1. **No Grumbling**. Mentoring sessions aren't bitch sessions about the company, management or customers. They need to be positive and offer a place to discuss challenges and ideas for overcoming them.

2. **What's the Goal?** It's essential for all parties to understand up front what the mentoring program is meant to achieve— what the goals and objectives are for both the new and experienced salespeople.

3. **Volunteer**. The mentors must want to do this. If they are being forced to mentor by management, there will be little buy-in from them, and the new salespeople will feel like they are wasting the time of the experienced person.

4. **It's not my way or the highway**. The mentor isn't there to dictate how the salesperson should do their job nor to clone the mentor's style of selling. The mentor is there to offer support and feedback that can help the new salesperson's own unique skills and talents.

Mentoring gives experienced salespeople a sense of accomplishment beyond their own sales. It gives them an opportunity to help someone else, and for most people, this feels good. For the new salesperson, it makes available someone who they do not directly report to as a sounding board and voice of reason and advice. It can be difficult or awkward for a new salesperson to confess ignorance by asking questions, especially personal ones, of their manager. Mentoring can be a win-win for the organization as long as you have the right people as mentors. Not every salesperson will be willing or able to do the job.

Coaching

In many sales organizations, the sales managers also do sales coaching, which can be a very difficult balancing act. The sales manager wears a manager hat when motivating and directing the salesperson to achieve goals. Coaching requires the manager to switch hats, to put on a coach's hat, when training or otherwise help a salesperson find their own answers about how to best move forward. If an organization is going to provide coaching, I suggest it be done by someone outside the organization—or at least outside the sales team. Coaching can be one of the most important aspects of sales success. I've had the opportunity to coach hundreds of salespeople. Coaching can be very rewarding for the organization and the salesperson, but there can be pitfalls if it's not set up and communicated properly. Here are a few points to consider:

1. **What is coaching meant to achieve?** A good coach should be one that asks hard questions of the salesperson and then guides them to find the answers themselves using their personal strengths and talents in balance. Good coaching can lead to amazing success, but it takes time.

2. **Who is doing the coaching?** The best coaching should come either from outside the organization using a professional coach or from a manager from a completely different sales team within the organization. If you are using someone on the inside, it's critical that they get trained on how

to be a good coach. Without training, they can cause more harm than good.

3. **Receptivity to Coaching**. The salesperson must be open to being coached. I have found that many top salespeople don't really want coaching because they think they already have all the answers, which, of course, is never true. I have found the most receptivity with salespeople in the middle of the pack who are looking to move to the next level of success.

4. **A good coach doesn't have all the answers**. But a good coach should have all the right questions. The coach's role is to guide the salesperson to find their *own* answers. The coach should be aware of the salesperson's strengths and talents and be able to connect those with the challenges that the salesperson is facing.

Most salespeople want coaching. Several years ago, Gallup found that 64 percent of salespeople wanted help from a coach. Almost every great salesperson I've known has had a coach at some point in their career, just as every great athlete attributes their success to their coaches.

Using the manager as coach

In the event your organization is going to use sales managers as coaches, there are some guidelines to keep in mind. I'm a fly fisherman, and in fly fishing, you don't just show up at a stream and throw a line in. You first study the water, how it is moving, what kinds of bugs are flying over and around it, whether there are fish surfacing in the water, and which direction the current is moving.

The first step as a manager/coach is understanding where each salesperson is in their job at that given moment. Maybe they're coming off the loss of a big sale and feeling depressed, or maybe it's the opposite. Maybe they're on a high because of sustained success. If you study the salesperson first, you can then determine what the next step in coaching should be for that salesperson. Do they need some cheerleading to get over that big loss? Some encouragement about how to move forward? Maybe they need to be brought down a little to keep a more even keel. The key is that you have to take the manager's hat off and put on the coach's hat.

To be an effective coach requires asking good, relevant questions and then shutting up to actively listen to the answers. Because many managers have come from being good salespeople themselves, this is a hard transition to make. Managers generally want to have all the answers. A good coach doesn't. As I said earlier, a coach guides the salesperson through the process of finding their own answers.

In the book *The Coaching Effect* by Bill Eckstrom and Sara Wirth, the authors write about the movie *Moneyball*, which is about how the Oakland Athletics baseball team completely flipped on its head baseball and the process of building a baseball team. Here's what they say about coaching:

These days, sales departments could learn a lot from the Moneyball example. They are mired in order. Their performance thinking is medieval and archaic, and there is an "epidemic failure" to understand what creates growth. Why is it that a team can underachieve and then bring in a new coach and achieve significant growth? They altered the input that has the most powerful impact on performance outcomes—the coach. Yet in business nobody quantifies coaching effectiveness. Executive leaders have forever been viewing incomplete or inaccurate data regarding team performance because they are not looking at the root cause of performance growth-the coach. This is the business version of Moneyball. Every CRM adoption, every technology implementation, all frontline employee and sales training, and anything and everything geared to helping employees become more productive should cease. No more resources should be committed to any frontline workers before the company understands the effectiveness of the coach. Until that happens, the success or failure of any programs, products or services

> cannot be accurately measured and under-
> stood without knowing if the coach enables or
> disables performance.

The authors say that when salespeople are elevated to managing, they often aren't given the tools and training to act as coaches versus managers. They're given a team and goals and then told to *go get 'em*! When the sales manager is the coach, there needs to be very specific support to help them become coaches.

The role of the manager

The sales manager can make or break a salesperson, not to mention an entire organization. Many companies promote their best salespeople to roles of leadership and sales management. This rarely leads to success. When the best salespeople move into sales management, they often do it for the wrong reasons: more money, more responsibility, more visibility in the organization. In other words, the decision to move into management is all about them.

The best sales managers take a very different view. They are good leaders first, meaning they want to serve and get the best out of their people. Inevitably, they will need to manage results, but if they give their people the tools they need, allow them to use their best strengths and talents and have a process for achieving results, the manager is simply helping and encouraging the salesperson to stay on track—with an occasional nudge to get back on track. The best sales managers don't have all the answers and don't dictate to salespeople how to do things based on the way they did things.

When a salesperson transitions to sales management, that person will need to use a completely different skill set than what made them a successful salesperson. It takes time to understand each team member, learn their strengths and talents and what makes them tick. A sales manager will be required to understand each person's strengths and talents and develop them in the best possible ways to help them achieve success. No salesperson will do jobs exactly as the sales manager did his or her sales job. Salespeople will do what they believe is the best way for them to achieve success, and at times the manager will be required to gently guide them back on track.

In the book *Discover Your Sales Strengths*, authors Tony Rutigliano and Bensen Smith lay out the following principles for sales manager success:

- **Rehire your best people**. This means reconnecting with the people that you can't afford to lose, reassuring them that you want them to continue what has made them successful.

- **Appreciate Uniqueness**. As I said earlier, understand that your salespeople are not going to do things the way you did them as a salesperson. Give them latitude to do it their way.

- **Lead from Strength**. Average managers believe that everyone should be treated equally. Leading-from-strength managers match talent with opportunities and resources.

- **Be a Buffer**. As a sales manager, you will occupy a space between the salesperson and the company. Don't fall into the trap of blaming the home office and grumbling in front of the sales team. Help salespeople understand the company's reasoning for its decisions, but don't hesitate to "go to bat" for your salespeople when necessary.

- **Hire the Best**. When you have the opportunity to hire, make sure you hire the best possible person. Don't worry so much about the resumé. Understand the person— their strengths, talents and abilities.

As a sales manager, you will have many opportunities to turn average salespeople into great salespeople. How well you do that will be how you are ultimately measured.

Questions to ask yourself

1. Do you have a mentor, and if so, do you know someone that might make a good mentor in your organization?

2. Have you considered coaching? How do you think a coach could help you achieve your vision?

3. As a sales manager, have you invested the time to understand your people and connect with them based on their strengths and talents?

Chapter 12
On Compensation, Motivation and Incentives

It's finally time to talk about motivation. Most sales organizations still believe that great salespeople are motivated principally by money. I would argue that most *organizations* are money-motivated, but that doesn't mean their salespeople are. In fact, if you look at the studies on motivation over the past twenty years, it becomes apparent that money is not a key motivator. Gallup has been doing surveys of employees for many years, and what they find—even now, during the Great Resignation—is that most people are not motivated by money. Money ranks about sixth on the list of what is most important in people's work.

Most sales organizations use the same method to motivate their salespeople as they did a hundred years ago—the carrot and the stick. This means that if you have successful results, you will be rewarded (the carrot), and if not, you will be punished (the stick). In Daniel Pink's book *Drive*, he identifies the three primary motivators for employees today—autonomy, mastery, and meaning and purpose. Let's look at how these three motivators work with salespeople.

Autonomy

Most salespeople prefer to work on their own and profoundly dislike anyone micro-managing them. In fact, micromanaging is one of the leading causes of mental health problems in salespeople, most of whom want to manage their own schedule, how they work with customers and how they do their work in general. I have talked with countless salespeople that dread their sales manager riding along with them for a day or two. They don't want the sales manager looking over their shoulder.

Autonomy means we let people do the job they need to do without a lot of supervision but with the tools they need to be successful. Does this idea of autonomy work? Daniel Pink wrote this about a study at Cornell University that:

...studied 320 small businesses, half of which granted workers autonomy and the other half relying on top-down direction. The businesses that offered autonomy grew at four times the rate of the control-oriented firms and had one-third the turnover.

Unfortunately, most sales organizations are managed from the top down. Sales goals are set by someone else and then driven by sales managers. What these organizations don't understand is that if they have the right salesperson and give them the autonomy to do his or her job, that salesperson will typically out-produce the top-down goals that were set by others. Too many sales organizations confuse activity with accomplishment.

Mastery

Most employees want to do the best job they can but are not given the training, support and tools needed to master their work. Salespeople are no different. They want to be successful. They want to be the best at what they do. And if they don't, they probably won't be in sales very long.

Mastery is not a concept only for top-producing salespersons. Mastery means that the salespeople execute their role to the best of their ability and consider the customer and their organization before themselves. Salespeople that have mastery are also typically very good at deep focus, which we talked about in the Rule of Excellence. When working in deep focus, they move into an area of mastery called flow. Think of the last time you did something where you were so engaged in it that you lost track of time. That's flow! You will often hear athletes talk about being in the zone. That is flow—that is mastery.

Another aspect of mastery is having the right mindset—figuring out what you want to be really good at. Once you understand that, you can begin to create flow. One of the things I really enjoy about my work is teaching, and I can often get into a state of flow when I'm developing new workshops and programs.

For salespeople wanting mastery and flow, it's about being the best at the process and doing the best for their customers. Mastery, however, is hard work. NBA Hall of Famer Julius Irving said, "Being a professional is doing the things you love to do on the days you don't feel like doing them."

Mastery demands constant work and practice. You must commit to your vocation of selling the same way a professional athlete commits to practice.

Purpose and meaning

We've talked about this in the Rule of Purpose and Vision, but the more a salesperson can connect their jobs to something greater than themselves, the better at it they will be. Understanding why we do what we do and why the company does what it does is vital to success. Most successful salespeople don't do their jobs just to make the most possible money for the company but rather to connect customer needs with solutions and build long-term relationships. This provides purpose and meaning to a sales career.

The idea of compensation as motivation

For decades, commission sales have been a staple of most sales organizations. In many sales positions, it is the only option. But for those people employed by organizations, the idea that you hire salespeople based on their money motivation is quickly becoming prehistoric thinking.

Most people under the age of forty-five are not motivated by money, as we have learned. In fact, there is very compelling evidence that when put in that type of environment, a salesperson can become more unmotivated. The same thing goes for rewards such as bonuses and incentives. Alfie Kohn, a researcher and author of one of the top books on rewards, *Punished by Rewards*, wrote this:

> The core of popular behaviorism is "Do this and you'll get that." The wisdom of this technique is very rarely held up for inspection; all that is open to question is what exactly people will receive and under what circumstances it

will be promised and delivered. We take for granted that this is a logical way to raise children, teach students and manage employees. We promise bubble gum to a 5-year-old if he behaves in the supermarket. We dangle an A before a teenager to get her to study harder and we hold out the possibility of a Hawaiian vacation for a salesperson who sells enough of a company's products.… My premise here is that rewarding people for their compliance is not "the way the world works," as many insist. It is not a fundamental law of human nature. It is but one way of thinking and speaking, of organizing our experience and dealing with others. It may seem natural to us, but it actually reflects a particular ideology that can be questioned. I believe it is long past time for us to do so. The steep price we pay for our uncritical allegiance to the use of rewards is what makes this story not only intriguing but also deeply disconcerting.

Kohn's book is a treatise on the idea that rewards don't work. Daniel Pink's book *Drive* shows that the carrot-and-stick method of motivation doesn't work. Yet here we are still using methods of compensation and rewards the same way we've done them for decades.

I don't profess to have all the answers, but as we look at the selling profession and its turnover and mental health issues, it would seem logical to question everything about the profession—certainly compensation and reward. Are there better ways? I believe there are, and they could be a variety of hybrids that combine elements of the old way with some newer experimental methods.

Questions to ask yourself

1. How are you motivating yourself or your salespeople?

2. Are your salespeople engaged?

3. How might you re-think the way you are motivating yourself and/or your salespeople?

Chapter 13
Final Thoughts

I know this book is a contrary view to the way most businesses and sales organizations have operated over many decades. But I challenge you to ask yourself these questions:

- Is what I or we are doing the best possible way to sell?

- Have I ever considered a different approach?

- What if a change could boost our sales 25 percent. Would change be worth it?

- Would loyal, happy salespeople be an asset to our business?

In the Rule of Excellence, I mentioned Adam Grant's book *Think Again*, in which the author writes about rethinking and suggests that we should think like a philosopher or a scientist. Scientific thinking begins with doubting what we already know, which leads to curiosity and looking at things differently. There must also be humility (one of Benedict's favorite topics), which reminds us that we don't know everything, and that, in turn, leads to the discovery of new ways of doing things. The way you rethink your sales systems is vital to making the changes needed in this new world of selling, which is so volatile, uncertain, complex and ambiguous.

I hope I've given you ideas to get you rethinking. What I have offered in this book is a comprehensive approach to selling, covering all aspects of sales success. You can certainly focus only on certain parts of the book and make incremental changes, but if you implement these ideas as a complete system, you will see a transformation. Whether it's you as a salesperson or your organization, you will see results that will not only impact sales but also percolate to all parts of the organization. If you are reading this book as an individual salesperson who doesn't have much control over what the organization tells you to do, you can implement these ideas on your own. Simply incorporate them into the activities you are already required to do. And when your sales manager realizes the success you're having, maybe the organization will become interested in how you did it.

The Rule of Benedict offers a blueprint for living and working in community. It gives us principles that work in almost every walk of life. In Judith Valente's book on the Rule *How To Live*, she writes:

> The Rule of Benedict invites an alternative vision. It is summed up in a single line form one of the shortest chapters in The Rule: The Good Zeal of Monastics, "Try to be the first to show respect to the other, supporting with the greatest patience one another's weaknesses or body and behavior. This is the good St. Benedict saying we are called to model. He asks us to nurture it zealously, with fervent love."

If those of us in sales just used that one piece of advice from the Rule, our lives and work would be better, and we would be on the road to flourishing.

Lastly, I want to talk briefly about faith. Benedict was Catholic, but the Rule and its principles are not necessarily Catholic. In fact, you can find Benedictine communities in almost every faith and religion. But Benedict does point to doing things for a higher purpose, and that purpose is to get us closer to salvation.

In my three decades of selling and helping others sell that higher purpose, my Catholic faith has been the foundation for my work, the way I treat people and certainly my success. The times when I have strayed away from that faith are usually the times when I have struggled. We can complete all the steps I've laid out in this book and still fail. Benedict addresses this in the prologue of his Rule:

What is not possible to us by nature, let us ask the Lord to supply by the help of his grace. (P:41)

We must have faith that a higher purpose, or whatever you may call it, exists, and if we keep our gaze focused on that higher power, we cannot fail. So go forth armed with these principles founded 1,500 years ago and use them to flourish in your work and make the world a better place.

If you would like to find ideas on how to implement these ideas as well as resources from the book, visit me at www.principledflourishing.com. I wish you the best Selling Like a Monk!

About the Author

As an executive coach, consultant and trainer, Mike has worked in over forty different industries. He is trained in Gallup StrengthsFinder, Values in Action Inventory, Virtuous Leadership, Positive Organizational Development and has a certificate in Positive Psychology. Mike has traveled throughout the country speaking to and working with business owners, Fortune 500 companies, non-profits, boards, churches and the US Military to help them implement the strategic planning process that he wrote about in his first book. In addition, Mike has worked with thousands of salespeople through training workshops and one-on-one coaching and has developed sales training programs for dozens of sales organizations.

Today, as founder and CEO of Principled Flourishing Group, Mike works with businesses, government, nonprofits and the church, focusing on strategic planning, positive organizational development, innovation, leadership and sales development. He also serves as the Director of Professional Development at the Benedictine Leadership Institute at Mt. Marty University in Yankton, South Dakota, creating and facilitating programs on leadership and innovation based on the timeless principles of the Benedictine tradition. In addition, he is a Benedictine Oblate, living out the principles from the Rule of Benedict.

In addition to this book, Mike has authored two other books, *Ultimate Breakthrough Planning: The Business Funnel Approach* and *Sweet Spot: Where Business Strategy, Positive Psychology and Faith Principles Converge*. He lives with his wife Anne in Sioux Falls, South Dakota.

Resources

Here is a list of resources that are mentioned that are great resources for the Monk Principles.

Chapter 1

- *The Rule of St. Benedict* in English by Timothy Fry, OSB

- *The Happiness Advantage* by Shawn Achor

- *Atomic Habits* by James Clear

- *To Sell is Human* by Daniel Pink

- *Good To Great* by Jim Collins

Chapter 2

- *The New Conceptual Selling* by Robert Miller and Stephen Heiman

- *The New Strategic Selling* by Robert Miller and Stephen Heiman

- *Virtuous Leadership* by Alexander Havard
- *The Seven Habits of Highly Effective People* by Steven Covey

Chapter 3

- *Grit: The Power of Passion and Perseverance* by Angela Duckworth
- *Start With Why* by Simon Sinek
- TEDX Talk: "The Golden Circle" by Simon Sinek
- *The Invisible Leader* by Zach Mercurio
- *As a Man Thinketh* by James Allen
- *Economics of a Higher Purpose* by Robert Quinn
- *Inner Game of Selling* by Ron Willingham
- *Nine Lies About Work* by Marcus Buckingham

Chapter 4

- *Character Strengths and Virtues* by Martin Seligman and Christopher Peterson
- *Power of Character Strengths* by Ryan Niemac
- *Grit: The Power of Passion and Perseverance* by Angela Duckworth

- *Good to Great* by Jim Collins

Chapter 5

- *Now Discover Your Strengths* by Donald Clifton and Marcus Buckingham
- *Strengths Based Selling* by Tony Rutigliano and Brian Brim

Chapter 6

- *Deep Work* by Cal Newport
- *Hero of a Thousand Faces* by Joseph Campbell
- *Story Brand* by Donald Miller
- *Think Again* by Adam Grant
- *Lean Startup* by Eric Ries
- *Value Proposition Design: How to Create Products and Services Customers Want* by Osterwalder, et al

Chapter 7

- *Wisdom Distilled from the Daily: Living The Rule of St. Benedict* by Joan Chittesler

Chapter 8

- *St. Benedict's Toolbox* by Jane Tomaine

Chapter 9

- *Unreasonable Hospitality* by Will Guidara
- *Setting the Table* by Danny Meyer

Chapter 10

- *Ultimate Breakthrough Planning: The Business Funnel Approach* by Mike Ferrell

Chapter 11

- *The Coaching Effect* by Bill Eckstrom and Sarah Wirth
- *Discover Your Sales Strengths* by Benson Smith and Tony Rutigliano

Chapter 12

- *Drive* by Daniel Pink
- *Punished By Rewards* by Alfie Kohn
- *How to Live* by Judith Valente